Ask the
Namibian Guides

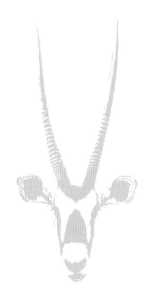

Ask the
Namibian Guides

by
Diana Rupp

SAFARI PRESS INC.

Rupp, Diana

First edition

Safari Press

2013 Long Beach, California

ISBN 978-1-57157-364-3

Library of Congress Catalog Card Number: 2010939013

10 9 8 7 6 5 4 3 2 1

Printed in China

Readers wishing to receive the Safari Press catalog, featuring many fine books on big-game hunting, wingshooting, and sporting firearms, should write to Safari Press Inc., P.O. Box 3095, Long Beach, CA 90803, USA. Tel: (714) 894-9080 or visit our Web site at www.safaripress.com.

This book is dedicated to
Namibia's outstanding professional hunters.
Thank you for making possible
the adventures
we safari hunters will never forget.

Table of Contents

Foreword

Jack Atcheson and Sons has always taken the research and development of great African hunting areas seriously. While East African hunting areas were well known by the 1960s, the development of hunting in southern Africa was just evolving in the early 1970s. Around that time, we were told about a region where kudu bull sightings could exceed thirty or more bulls a day—a region that held many bulls whose horns were in excess of fifty inches in length! Kudu hunting in the safari destinations of that era were very good, but on a fourteen-day safari one might see only a handful of kudu bulls, and a fifty-inch-class bull was truly rare. We had to know more!

We, therefore, enlisted one of our favorite critics of great hunting, the late Jack O'Connor, to go and have a good look. Jack embarked with his family in tow to South-West Africa, or, as we know it now, Namibia. Jack hunted with Volker Grellmann of Anvo Hunting Safaris, and upon his return his glowing report confirmed the stories of abundant and huge spiral-horned kudu bulls. Eleanor O'Connor took a sixty-inch bull, and the rest of the O'Connor family took bulls with horns in the mid-fifties.

Jack spoke about the beauty of the land, from mountains to endless savannas, the friendly people, and the quality of the game. We went to work on spreading the news, and since then the Atcheson clan has been introducing hunters to Namibia for over forty years. The hunting scene just gets better and better!

Namibia is one of the few areas in Africa where a safari for the Big Five can still take place. This is a very big deal! There are still many huge kudus, and a few hundred-plus-pound tuskers have been taken recently. The country offers some of Africa's best leopard hunting. Big antelope species like roan and sable are increasing. Rarities like red lechwe, Damara dik-dik, and sitatunga are open to limited hunting.

Some years ago, the government of Namibia formed the Namibian Association of Community Based Natural Resource Management (NASCO). This led to the development of fifty-nine tribally owned conservancies in which the local wildlife resources are managed by professional wildlife managers and leased to professional hunting companies, and the camps are staffed by local trackers, camp managers, and workers. Some of these conservancies cover millions of acres of undeveloped wild lands, much like the prime game areas of East Africa. The wildlife has taken on new meaning to local people, and it is flourishing!

On private lands much of the same has occurred. Namibia is covered in endless rich savanna grasslands, and cattlemen have developed water projects for cattle that have greatly benefited wildlife. I visited the minister of Environment, the Honorable N. Nandi-Ndaitwah, in June 2010, and she assured me that Namibia is committed to helping its rural people and wildlife resources to coexist, and hunting will play a major part.

I am really pleased to see a book written to spread awareness of what a great safari destination Namibia is for today's sportsmen. Don't forget to take your family!

Jack Atcheson Jr.
Butte, Montana
February 2011

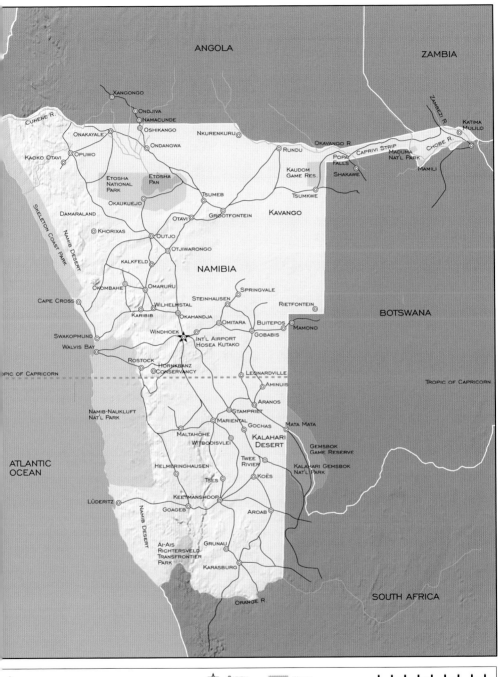

ANGOLA

ZAMBIA

XANGONGO

CUNENE R.

ONDJIVA

NAMACUNDE

OSHIKANGO

KATIMA
MULILO

ZAMBEZI R.

ONAKAYALE

NKURENKURU

OKAVANGO R.

CHOBE R.

CAPRIVI STRIP

MADUMA
NAT'L PARK

ONDANGWA

RUNDU

MAMILI

KAOKO OTAVI

OPUWO

POPA
FALLS

KAUDOM
GAME RES.

SHAKAWE

SKELETON COAST PARK

ETOSHA
NATIONAL
PARK

ETOSHA
PAN

TSUMEB

TSUMKWE

OKAUKUEJO

NAMIB DESERT

DAMARALAND

GROOTFONTEIN

KAVANGO

KHORIXAS

OTAVI

OUTJO

OTJIWARONGO

KALKFELD

NAMIBIA

OKOMBAHE

OMARURU

SPRINGVALE

STEINHAUSEN

RIETFONTEIN

BOTSWANA

CAPE CROSS

WILHELMSTAL

KARIBIB

OKAHANDJA

OMITARA

BUITEPOS

MAMONO

SWAKOPMUND

WINDHOEK

INT'L AIRPORT
HOSEA KUTAKO

GOBABIS

WALVIS BAY

ROSTOCK

HORNKRANZ
CONSERVANCY

TROPIC OF CAPRICORN

LEONARDVILLE

TROPIC OF CAPRICORN

AMINUIS

ARANOS

NAMIB-NAUKLUFT
NAT'L PARK

STAMPRIET

MARIENTAL

GOCHAS

MATA MATA

MALTAHÖHE

KALAHARI
DESERT

WITBOOISVLEI

GEMSBOK
GAME RESERVE

ATLANTIC
OCEAN

HELMERINGHAUSEN

TWEE
RIVIER

KALAHARI GEMSBOK
NAT'L PARK

TSES

KOËS

LÜDERITZ

NAMIB DESERT

KEETMANSHOOP

GOAGEB

AROAB

AI-AIS
RICHTERSVELD
TRANSFRONTIER
PARK

GRUNAU

KARASBURG

SOUTH AFRICA

ORANGE R.

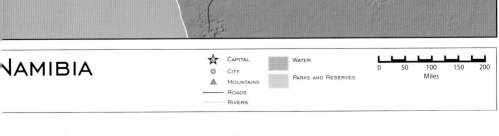

NAMIBIA

★ CAPITAL
◎ CITY
▲ MOUNTAINS
— ROADS
···· RIVERS

WATER

PARKS AND RESERVES

0   50   100   150   200
Miles

Introduction

Chapter 1

Of all the amazing animals I saw in the wild on my first African safari, the red hartebeest was the biggest surprise. In photos, these animals look somewhat odd and ungainly, with long, narrow faces and oversized chests and shoulders. But the first time I saw several hartebeests moving across a dusty plain in central Namibia, the sight of them took my breath away. Their coats were a lovely burnished copper, and the dark markings on their faces and black, bent-back horns were a stunning contrast to the red bodies. Nor were they ungainly—they were graceful and beautiful, and as I watched them loping through the African landscape, I could see how perfectly adapted they were to the landscape of central Namibia, its sun-drenched plains scattered with thorn trees, low bushes, and rocky hills called kopjes.

During the midday hours, hunters often take a lunch break overlooking a water hole, just to watch and photograph the wildlife that comes to drink. (Photo by J. Scott Rupp)

Ask the Namibian Guides

Diana and Scott Rupp with the two red hartebeest they shot within minutes of each other.

In over a week of hunting, I had the chance to stalk numerous hartebeests, but it seemed that in addition to their other qualities, these animals had eyes on the backs of their heads, for they gave us the slip every time. In the meantime, though, my husband, Scott, and I and our PH, Johan, were having a wonderful time, glassing giraffe and zebra, and proudly putting our first African game kills—warthog, gemsbok, and springbok—in the salt shed.

On the second-to-last day of hunting, just as the morning chill was giving way to another dry, warm day, we followed our tracker and PH as they scrambled up jumbled red boulders covered with sparse grass to the peak of a kopje, which gave us a fine view of the surrounding terrain. The four of us lay prone atop the outcropping, glassing, when four very impressive hartebeest bulls came trotting into view around the base of the kopje.

We lay still, awaiting our opportunity, and when the hartebeest fed to within 150 yards of our position, Scott dropped the largest one with a shot from his .300 WSM. Amazingly, the other three remained, milling around in some confusion, and that gave me the opportunity to crawl up beside Johan, find

Introduction

another large bull in my scope, and drop him as well. Scott and I have hunted together a lot, but to this day those hartebeest remain our only "double"—and we could not have been more thrilled with our two outstanding trophies or the experience of an exciting hunt in an exotic land.

It was later that same day that I found myself kneeling next to my most sought-after African trophy, experiencing a dream come true. After a heart-pounding stalk through thick brush, Johan and I had sneaked to within eighty yards of a greater kudu, and after a well-placed shot from the shooting sticks I was tracing the ridges of the curling horns of my magnificent fifty-inch kudu bull. The memories of that day still remain sharply etched in my mind: not just the kudu's curling horns and white-striped hide, but the dust in my clothes and the thorn cuts on my hands; the go-away bird calling from a nearby tree as we took photos; and the welcome taste of a cold Coca-Cola from the ice box slaking my thirst.

They say your first African safari is a life-changing experience. It certainly was for me, and I feel especially fortunate that I chose what I still believe to be the perfect country for a neophyte's introduction to Africa. The thornbrush

The author with the animal she most wanted when she came to Namibia—a greater kudu. (Photo by J. Scott Rupp)

savanna of Namibia's central plateau teems with game—warthog, gemsbok, giraffe, kudu, and hartebeest especially, and everywhere I looked, there was something new to discover. From the communal nests of the sociable weaver bird, which looked heavy enough to topple the trees that held them, to mysterious, ancient paintings of ostriches and antelopes adorning the walls of a rocky canyon, the memories of the Namibian countryside are indelibly etched into my mind.

On day two of that safari I wrote this in my journal: *It was blazing hot all day, and then the second it got dark it became really cold riding in that open Land Cruiser, and I threw on a fleece jacket, warm hat, and gloves. But as we headed back to the lodge, the Southern Cross and a zillion other stars and the Milky Way were gleaming brightly in a sky absolutely untouched by any light anywhere. It was spectacular.*

The Country

Namibia does not necessarily invite comparisons to the broad, lush savannas of East Africa famously depicted in *Out of Africa,* nor does it possess jungles that bring to mind Tarzan. Namibia, located on Africa's west coast, is a land of great contrasts, with dunes and deserts in the west, semidesert plains in the central regions, rugged mountains in the south, and even forests and swamps in the far northeast. Its incredibly dark nights and bright stars make sense when you consider that this is a nation of 317,816 square miles, larger than the state of Texas, with a fairly sparse human population of some two million people (about 6.5 people per square mile). It has some forty-two huntable species of game available, including all the Big Five—lion, leopard, elephant, buffalo, and rhino—and some outstanding bird hunting, to boot.

Namibia is bordered by the Atlantic Ocean on the west, Angola on the north, Botswana on the east, and South Africa on the east and south. A thin panhandle of land, known as the Caprivi Strip, stretches out from the northeastern corner like a pointed finger, and here the country's borders touch Zambia to the north and Zimbabwe to the east. The Caprivi Strip and the region just south of it, known as the Kavango, are the rainiest areas of the country, flat and covered with dense bushveld. This northern region is where the majority of the country's buffalo and elephant hunting takes place.

Most of the country's population—and many of its plains-game and leopard-hunting areas, including the site of my own first safari—are in the

Introduction

central plateau, where elevations range from 3,600 feet to some 6,000 feet. This is also the location of the capital city, Windhoek. East and west of this plateau are spectacular desert areas.

The Namib Desert on the west is a relatively narrow belt that runs the entire length of the country along its coastline, and is known for its magnificent sand dunes. The Namib region includes Namib-Naukluft National Park, the tourist region of Swakopmund, the Skeleton Coast, and Damaraland in the northwest. Then there is the Kalahari Desert on the east, which is known for its long strips of dunes and excellent populations of gemsbok and springbok.

Unsurprisingly for a country comprised largely of desert and semidesert, Namibia boasts a lot of sunshine—some 300 days a year are sunny, on average. Summer (November through March) is the rainy season, and during that time 20 to 28 inches of rain may fall in the northeast, 12 to 20 in the central highlands, and often less than two inches in the western deserts. Average temperatures in

The night skies in Namibia are unforgettable. (Photo courtesy of Joof Lamprecht)

the winter months, when most hunting is done, are 77 degrees F at midday and 32 at night. In summer it may be 104 at midday and 77 at night.

Although its human population is relatively low, Namibia is an extremely diverse country. Most Namibians fall into one of eleven ethnic groups, including the San, Nama, Khoi-Khoi, Herero, Himba, Kavango, Tswana, Caprivian, Ovambo, Damara, and Rehoboth Baster peoples. Some 15 percent of the population is of European descent, primarily Germans, Portuguese, and Afrikaners, and there is a significant Asian minority as well. English is the official language, but German, Afrikaans, and indigenous languages are widely spoken.

Namibia was a German protectorate, known as South-West Africa (or German South-West Africa) beginning in the 1880s. However, after World War I, South Africa was given a mandate to administer the territory, which continued until the country officially became independent in 1991, making it the last country in Africa to gain independence.

Namibia has excellent infrastructure, among the best in Africa. It boasts 19,885 miles of paved and gravel roads, and most are well maintained. The major international airport, known variously as Hosea Kutako International Airport or Windhoek International Airport, is located twenty-six miles east of the capital city of Windhoek. It has regular air service from Johannesburg, Frankfurt, and London. There is a good network of telephone landlines throughout the country, and most towns have cell phone coverage.

The majority of the country—the south, east, west, and central regions—are malaria free, as there are no mosquitoes to speak of. However, if traveling or hunting in the northwestern or northeastern areas of the country, malaria prophylaxis is recommended. Otherwise, no inoculations are required, but when traveling to Africa it's always a good idea to get shots for yellow fever, meningitis, and hepatitis A and B.

The Hunting

As a whole, Namibia offers close to fifty huntable game animals, although not all types are found in every area of the country. In addition, not all of these animals are actually indigenous to the country; many have been imported for breeding on game farms, where huntable populations have been established. Namibia does have a number of indigenous species that are available nowhere else in Africa, including the Hartmann mountain zebra, the Damara dik-dik, and the black-faced impala. Namibia is also the only country that has a CITES quota for cheetah. However, it's important to note that although both black-faced impala

A giraffe pauses for a drink. (Photo courtesy of Jofie Lamprecht)

Namibia has a large leopard population, and the cats are hunted in many areas of the country. (Photo courtesy of Dirk DeBod)

and cheetah can be legally hunted in Namibia, these trophies cannot be imported into the United States.

Animals officially listed as "available on license" in Namibia are: baboon, blesbok, Cape buffalo, Chobe bushbuck, bushpig, caracal, civet, cheetah, Nile crocodile, Damara dik-dik, southern bush duiker, Cape eland, elephant, Kalahari gemsbok, genet, giraffe, red hartebeest, hippo, brown hyena, spotted hyena, black-faced impala, southern impala, black-backed jackal, klipspringer, southern greater kudu, red lechwe, leopard, lion, nyala, oribi, ostrich, porcupine, southern roan, common reedbuck, black rhino, white rhino, common sable, serval, Zambezi sitatunga, Kalahari springbok, steenbok, tsessebe, warthog, common waterbuck, Angolan defassa waterbuck, wildcat, black wildebeest, blue wildebeest, Burchell (plains) zebra, and Hartmann (mountain) zebra.

Bird shooting in Namibia, though often overlooked by hunters more focused on big game, is excellent. The country boasts a large diversity of game birds, including Namakwa dove, mourning dove, Cape turtle dove, Namakwa sand grouse, Burchell sand grouse, double banded sand grouse,

Introduction

red-billed francolin, Swainson francolin, guinea fowl, red billed teal, Egyptian geese, and spur-wing geese. In many cases, bird shooting can be combined with a big-game safari.

Hunting is controlled by two government agencies, the Ministry of Wildlife and Tourism (MET) and the Namibia Tourism Board, under which all professional hunters have to be registered. Namibia's requirements for registering professional hunters are quite strict. To receive the "professional hunter" designation, applicants must undergo a lengthy training regimen that requires them to become extremely knowledgeable about game and nongame wildlife. The qualification process includes passing several exams, both theoretical and practical. The entire process of becoming a fully registered PH can take up to four years.

The hunting season in Namibia begins 1 February and ends 30 November. All safari hunters must have a valid hunting permit from the MET specifying the species they intend to take, which your guide will obtain for you. Just make sure he has it when the hunt starts. A maximum of two animals of the same species may be taken on a safari on one hunting permit. Hunting hours are one-half hour before sunrise to one-half hour after sunset. It is illegal to hunt at night, or with an artificial light. Namibia's rules say that one guide may hunt with only two hunters at a time.

Namibia has an active and influential professional hunter's organization, the Namibian Professional Hunting Association (NAPHA). While professional hunters in Namibia are not required to be members of this organization, the vast majority of them are. NAPHA's Web site (www.natron.net/napha/) provides a listing of all its members along with contact information and other up-to-date information that is helpful to anyone considering hunting in Namibia.

In recent years Namibia has become one of the most popular destinations for safari hunters, both first-timers and old Africa hands alike. In 2007, Namibia hosted an estimated 6,100 international safari hunters, which makes it the second-most popular hunting country in Africa, after South Africa. Hunting takes place on many types of landscapes, including low-fenced livestock ranches, high-fenced game ranches, communal conservancies, government-owned concessions, and game reserves.

Ranches are generally privately owned or leased to the hunting operator. Communal conservancies are usually tribal areas where several communities have joined together to create a conservancy that must meet certain requirements and is then given its own hunting quota, with the local people as the stakeholders and beneficiaries of the hunting revenues. Currently, there are some fifty of these conservancies around the country, with more in development.

Importing guns into Namibia for hunting purposes is easy and hassle-free. A maximum of two firearms (rifles or shotguns only—no handguns or semiautomatic rifles) are allowed, along with sixty rounds of ammunition per rifle per hunter. (Shotgun shells can be purchased in the country if necessary.) An application form for the temporary import of firearms is available at the police booth at the airport and can be filled out upon arrival.

This is a simple process. You'll need to provide proof of ownership of the firearm by producing U.S. Customs Form 4457; your passport; home address; address where your hunt will be conducted; a return airline ticket; and the serial number and caliber of your firearm(s) and amount of ammunition. No permit is needed for bows; however, crossbows are not allowed.

About Professional Hunters

At the head of a safari, the hunter finally combines the duties of a sea captain, a bodyguard, a chauffeur, a tracker, a skinner, a headwaiter, a tourist guide, a photographer, a mechanic, a stevedore, an interpreter, a game expert, a gin-rummy partner, drinking companion, social equal, technical superior, boss, employee, and handy man. Robert C. Ruark, *Horn of the Hunter*

In Namibia, as in all of Africa, hunting guides are called professional hunters, or PHs. This is not just a term. African professional hunters are, indeed, professionals. This is especially true in Namibia, where the training requirements for aspiring PHs are especially stringent. In other places in the world, if you are unlucky, you may end up with a hunting guide who has little familiarity with area and the game. In Namibia, that is highly unlikely. The professionals who take hunters afield in this country are not only experts on the game animals, they will likely be able to identify every songbird you spot, tell you the scientific names of trees and other plants, expertly work your digital camera, whip up a delicious barbecue in the field, and probably talk knowledgeably with you on just about any subject you might wish to discuss.

When Robert Ruark wrote so glowingly in *Horn of the Hunter* of his African mentor, Harry Selby, he captured perfectly the way most safari hunters feel about their professional hunters. Professional hunters—the good ones, anyway, and almost all of the successful ones are good—are some of the most remarkable people

Introduction

you will ever meet. They must be all of the things that Ruark mentions—people able to get along well with clients from all walks of life. Anyone who has spent much time in hunting camps knows that hunting may bring out both the best and the worst in people, depending upon the hunter and how things go. Professional hunters, as a rule, are good at all of the things you hire them for—finding game, helping you get in position for a shot, helping you learn about and appreciate Africa—but they do much more behind the scenes, keeping their camps and the safari running smoothly, whether that means making emergency repairs to a Land Cruiser or soothing a client who has made a poor shot.

When your safari is finished, you will likely remember the good times you had with your PH as strongly as you remember your perfect shot on a gemsbok or the kudu that silhouetted itself on a ridge at last light. Conversely, choosing the wrong PH can mean that your safari is not as enjoyable as it could be—after all, personalities and safari goals differ, and a hunter whose goal is a leisurely safari will not be happy with a PH who hikes over hill and dale, and vice versa.

Highly sought-after plains game species such as the sable are increasing in numbers in Namibia, and are on license in many areas. (Photo courtesy of Dirk DeBod)

Scott Rupp with an outstanding warthog.

The author and professional hunter Johan Kotzé admire a nice springbok. (Photo by J. Scott Rupp)

Introduction

Sociable weaver birds build enormous nests that look as though they will topple the trees they are built in.

On a typical plains-game hunt, the hunting party drives slowly through the landscape in a four-wheel-drive vehicle, stopping frequently to glass for game. (Photo by J. Scott Rupp)

One of the many unusual animals you may see in Namibia—a Cape pangolin. (Photo courtesy of Diethelm Metzger)

My experience has been that, contrary to the old Gregory Peck-movie cliché, today's PHs are consummate professionals. The majority of them are family men with strong core values of honesty and fairness, and they will do everything in their power to ensure that you have an enjoyable and successful safari, often going far above and beyond the call of duty to do so. That said, it is also contingent upon you, the safari client, to know more or less what you're getting into. Of course, if you've never been on safari before or you've never been to a particular country, you can't know exactly what to expect. But you can do enough research to give yourself a general idea of what various PHs and outfits offer and how they do business, and try to find one that fits you the best. After that, you'll want to be open-minded and ready to live the adventure you've dreamed of for so long. As in any hunting, nothing on safari is guaranteed.

Introduction

You may not get exactly what you came for, but if my experience is any guide, you will, in the end, get much, much more.

The Ultimate Source

When I first started looking into traveling to Africa, I discovered that most of the information available was written by outdoor writers who did a good job of describing their own experiences, but often had little in-depth knowledge. I felt it would be more enlightening to speak with the real experts—established professional hunters who conduct dozens of safaris every year. Not only would they be the best sources of what a safari would really be like, they could give solid advice on what to bring, what to hunt, and what to actually expect. My goal was to get the information straight from the ultimate experts—the PHs themselves.

In these pages you'll hear from some of the top PHs in a country known for its outstanding hunting and expert guides. The PHs who were interviewed for this book are all long-established professionals representing a wide range of expertise: Some are plains-game experts and others are dangerous-game specialists. Some hunt on private farms; others hunt on wilderness concessions. While they may not always agree with each other on every point, the combined wisdom of these professionals will leave you with an excellent overview of what to expect from a safari in Namibia and how best to prepare for a hunting adventure in this magnificent country.

Once you've read their advice and suggestions I feel sure you'll be more confident about the experience you'll have in Namibia—and you'll doubtless be excited to visit, revisit, and hunt in this jewel of the Dark Continent.

Meet the Guides

Chapter 2

Tell us about yourself. How many years of experience do you have? How did you get started in the business? Give an overview of the species you hunt.

Janneman Brand
Kalahari Safari
www.kalahari-safari.com
info@kalahari-safari.com

Ever since I was a young boy living in Namibia and spending much of my time in the field, my dream was to utilize the family ranch in the Kalahari as a hunting destination. After completing my law degree and playing professional sports for a few years in South Africa and abroad, I made the decision to make my dream a reality.

My wife, Aldalene, and I returned to Namibia eight years ago, and with the grace of God, we have built Kalahari Safari into a successful hunting operation. Our family is the third Brand generation on the ranch. We are a family-run operation, situated on 35,000 acres of privately owned land in the Kalahari. Kalahari Safari specializes in plains-game safaris.

Meet the Guides

Dirk de Bod
Dirk de Bod Safaris Namibia
www.safarisnamibia.com
kudu@africaonline.com.na

I have been hunting in Namibia for the last twenty years for plains game and dangerous game. I have my own land on which we hunt a wide variety of plains game and leopard, and we hunt other species on concessions where I have exclusive hunting rights. I will do dangerous-game hunts upon request in concessions in the Caprivi.

I am the holder of the most top-ten trophies taken in the Namibia Professional Hunting Association record system today, as well as many in the SCI record books. I am a life member of the Dallas Safari Club, Safari Club International, NAPHA, and the African Professional Hunters Association.

I was raised on a cattle farm in northern Namibia where my father encouraged my passions for hunting, conservation, and nature. I graduated from school in 1982 and served in the Special Forces until 1989. In 1990, I bought a gun store in Windhoek and began my professional hunting career a few years later. By 1998, I had purchased my ranch and had begun to reintroduce the indigenous game. A year later, I sold the gun store to concentrate on professional hunting, game ranching, and being active in conservation and related projects.

I have been married to Rina for seventeen years and have a daughter and a son who share my passion for nature.

Kai-Uwe Denker
African Hunting Safaris
denkerk@iafrica.com.na

I grew up on a cattle ranch in eastern Namibia with plentiful free-roaming wildlife, so hunting has been a part of my life for as long as I can remember. I started off with a little air gun when I was four years old, was allowed to use a .22 when five, and shot my first springbok when I was twelve.

As a sideline to his cattle business, my father also accommodated visiting trophy hunters on our farm, so I naturally grew into the trophy hunting business. I guided the first clients on my father's farm in the late 1970s. In the 1980s I worked for various Namibian outfitters, and in 1989 I started my own safari company, African Hunting Safaris, which, together with my wife, Siggi, I still run today.

We hunt both dangerous and plains game, specializing in elephants, but we are also known for our hunts for indigenous Namibian plains game like greater kudu, springbok, gemsbok, and others.

Meet the Guides

Peter Kibble
Trophy Safaris
www.trophysafarisnamibia.us
trophysa@mweb.com.na

Born in 1945, I grew up in Kenya, East Africa. I learned about ethical hunting at an early age by spending my free time as a boy hunting and fishing at every opportunity. Schooling was definitely not on the agenda!

I spent many hours under the watchful eyes of some of Africa's great old-time hunters, including Eric Rundgren, John Cook, Bill Ryan, John Dugmore, John Lawrence, and Fred Bartlett, the author of *Shoot Straight and Stay Alive.* By 1962 I was hunting dangerous game, mainly problem animals like elephant, buffalo, and leopard.

In 1967 I married Liz, the daughter of Fred Bartlett. We have three sons, Michael, Kevin, and Brian, a new generation of professional hunters. Together we run a hunting, fishing, and photographic operation, and we pride ourselves on providing quality trophies and fair-chase hunting safaris.

Professional hunting and fishing are my passions, as they are for my sons. We hunt out of tented camps and spike camps on more than 1,000,000 acres in concessions that contain a variety of quality animals; we fish on the Kavango River for tigerfish, bream, and other species; and we conduct photographic safaris. We are very busy.

I work out of Windhoek, the capital city of Namibia, and have a semipermanent luxury tented camp 135 kilometers (84 miles) away. We hunt mainly plains game, and from time to time elephant, buffalo, lion, leopard, hippo, and crocodile. To hunt these we have to go north, a day's drive away.

Johan Kotzé
Doornfontein Hunting Lodge
www.dornfonteinhunting.com
info@dornfonteinsafaris.com

I was born in Namibia and also grew up in this beautiful country. From a very young age, I had the opportunity to go on hunting trips with my father, my family, and friends, and I was given the chance to hunt. After I finished school, I decided that, because of my love of nature and interest in hunting, I would like to become a professional hunter. We are very blessed in this country with such a large amount of farmland and concession areas where hunting can take place. I have been registered as a professional hunter since 2000 and have been hunting full-time since that time.

I started off hunting for Omatako Hunting Trails, still a well-known safari operator in Namibia. From there, I moved on to Erindi Hunting Safaris, which was later turned into a Nature Reserve. After that, I did a bit of guiding for Omujeve Hunting Safaris and Dirk de Bod, both very well-established outfitters in Namibia.

I got married in 2006 to Martie, and since then we have been working together at Doornfontein Hunting Lodge. She runs the lodge, does the administrative work, and is a master chef. We are blessed with a little boy, Christiaan, who was born in 2010.

At this stage, I have a license to guide clients only for plains game, but I think it is every PH's dream to move on to dangerous game. In Namibia, one needs a separate license in order to guide for these types of hunts, and I will be working on this qualification in the next couple of years.

Corne Kruger
Omujeve Safaris
www.omujevesafaris.com
info@omujevesafaris.com

I started hunting when I was four years old. That's when I got a pellet rifle from my grandfather. Both my grandfathers had ranches in the southern part of Namibia, and they played a big part in encouraging my interest in hunting. I spent every school holiday with them, and they taught me everything from shooting and gun safety to respect for wildlife. I owe my success to them.

From the time I was seven, other kids I knew were saying they wanted to be firemen and policemen. I always said, "I want to be a hunter!"

The teachers always asked me, "How are you going to make money doing that?" because the trophy hunting industry in Namibia back then was very small.

As I grew up, I did more and more hunting, and the passion just grew. In 2001, I got my professional hunter's license and started my career as a professional hunter at Erindi Private Game Reserve. When Erindi discontinued its hunting program in 2007, my family bought Omujeve Hunting Safaris, and ever since, we have been building the company into the largest hunting company in Namibia.

I have now been a professional hunter in Namibia for ten years. I have hunted both plains game and dangerous game during that time. I used to specialize in leopard hunts with hounds, until the government discontinued those hunts in 2010. Hunting with hounds, I guided clients to thirty-six leopards over a period of seven years.

Joof Lamprecht
Hunters Namibia Safaris
www.huntersnamibia.com
huntersn@mweb.com.na

I was born in Pretoria, South Africa, in 1948. Every spare moment of my youth was spent in the bush, hunting and exploring. I educated myself in the art of bushcraft and hunting, as none of my family members were outdoorsmen. At the age of twelve, I shot a leopard with only my Zulu hunting buddy of the same age at my side. This was a preview of life to come.

After finishing high school, I studied briefly at the Medical Faculty of Pretoria, but I decided that my future did not lie in medicine. I completed training in construction management at the University of the Witwatersrand and started my career in the building industry. I knew I could make a fortune in this field, which I could use to fulfill my lifelong dream of a career in trophy hunting and tourism, as well as to own my own piece of Africa. I started my own construction company at the age of twenty-five, after relocating to Namibia.

Four years later I met my wife-to-be, Marina, and we decided to sell the construction business to begin a career in the safari industry. In 1979, I qualified as a professional hunter, but after a three-year partnership in Omaruru Safaris I decided to go it alone, establishing Hunters Namibia Safaris soon thereafter. I decided that a sporting-goods store would complement the safari activities, so I established the very successful "The Gun Shop—Windhoek." Soon afterward we purchased Rooikraal Game Ranch. Through years of hard work and dedication to the wildlife, the environment, and the local community, we developed the land into one of southern Africa's most beautiful and game-rich areas.

I am passionate about sharing my love of and expertise in wildlife and hunting. My favorite challenge is introducing this magical continent to first-time hunters to Africa.

Meet the Guides

Willem Mans
KumKum Game Ranch
www.kumkum.com.na
hunting@kumkum.com.na

I was born in Kenhardt, South Africa, in 1943, and grew up on a sheep farm exactly 180 miles from where we live today. I hunted birds, hyraxes, hares, springhares, and the occasional steenbok—the only game available in those days—with dogs and a .22 Remington long rifle (still have it!). I hunted on my own from the time I was about eight years old.

I finished school at the famous Paarl Gymnasium and went on to Stellenbosch University where I obtained a bachelor's degree in commerce (1964). I started working with Ford in Port Elizabeth in the Eastern Cape, and married my university girlfriend in 1967—she was a well-known South African magazine's Bride of the Year, and she is still beautiful!

I obtained a business economics degree at Port Elizabeth University with part-time studies in 1968. In 1975 we bought our own retail business. After building a big new shop in 1983, we sold it in August 1987 to a very well-known public retail group. We had planned to do this, with the idea of going into game farming.

We bought KumKum Game Ranch twenty-three years ago, shortly after selling our retail business in 1987. I soon took the Namibian PH exams and started guiding trophy hunters from all over the world.

We have three kids, two girls and a boy; our son grew up hunting with me and is now a qualified professional hunter both in the RSA and in Namibia.

We hunt plains game and leopard, specializing in very good gemsbok, springbok, red hartebeest, and klipspringer, of which this area holds the best, on average, in all of southern Africa.

Ask the Namibian Guides

Diethelm Metzger
Makadi Safaris
www.makadi-safaris.com
diethelm@kamab-simbra.com

I was born in Windhoek, representing the fourth generation of Metzgers in Namibia. Growing up on my parents' ranch, hunting became my second nature. At age twelve I shot my first kudu bull with my dad's Mauser 8x68.

I studied at the University of Pretoria, South Africa, where I obtained a bachelor's degree in agricultural economics. This is also where Katja and I met. I then moved on to Texas A&M University to study for a master's degree in agricultural economics. During this time, Katja and I were married. We have three children: Tatjana, Aljoscha, and Nikolai.

My parents, Dieter and Ulla Metzger, started Makadi Safaris in 1972. This came about as quite a coincidence as trophy hunting had not yet been introduced to Namibia. In 1968, Bob Owen, an American, was visiting Namibia on business. One weekend, friends took him to my parents' property for a visit and a little bit of hunting. He and my dad went hunting and they shot a red hartebeest and a springbok. When Bob asked for a bill for the hunting, my father did not understand. He was quite content having meat in the locker. But Bob, having hunted in different African countries, explained to my father how the hunting business should work. After some discussions and a few letters written back and forth, they developed Makadi Safaris.

Katja and I joined the business as partners in 1990. Seven years later, my parents retired, and we continued to build the business. We now have three times as many hunting guests as we had twenty years ago. Makadi Safaris concentrates on good quality plains-game trophy hunts. This is our core business, although through business links to outfitters in several countries, we are able to offer big-game hunting opportunities as well.

Meet the Guides

Peter Thormählen
Thormählen & Cochran Safaris
www.africatrophyhunting.com
peter@africatrophyhunting.com

I am the cofounder and managing director of Thormählen & Cochran Safaris. I was born and raised in the Eastern Free State, South Africa. I speak German, Afrikaans, English, and Sotho fluently. After school I did two years of military service; during that time I became a commander and tracker for a Special Forces platoon, completing nine months of active war duty. Following military service, I attended university, where I completed a master's degree in organic soil chemistry and later a master's degree in business leadership (MBL).

After university I qualified as professional hunter, began hunting on a freelance basis, and started my own hunting company, Peter Thormählen Safaris, in a partnership with Hong Kong-based StradCom Holdings Ltd. This later led to the formation T&C Safaris South Africa and T&C Safaris Namibia.

I started hunting professionally in 1998. I had always wanted to become a professional hunter. I studied for my degrees because I wanted something to fall back on if needed. After I finished with my first master's degree in 1990, I bought a farm, which I sold in 1998. After I sold my farm, I freelanced as a professional hunter during the winter months to sustain my family, and during the summer months I worked as a landscaper, installing irrigation systems and instant lawns. I did this from 1998 until 2002, after which we started booking enough clients so that I hunted the whole time from April through November.

We hunt the whole spectrum of southern African plains game. I specialize in big buffalo, black rhino, and leopard. Cape buffalo and rhino are my passion, hence our company logo of a buffalo skull.

Jamy Traut
Jamy Traut Hunting Safaris
www.jamyhunt.com
jamytraut@gmail.com

I grew up for the most part on a farm in northeastern Namibia, where hunting was part of the routine. We did not hunt for trophies in those days, but still, a big kudu got your attention, even if he was only worth something in pounds and ounces of meat.

I went to school in the town of Grootfontein, living on a farm just outside of town, and my younger sister and I would ride to school on our bicycles every morning. In the semidarkness before dawn we would encounter kudu, eland, warthog, and other game. After high school, I studied basic sciences at the University of the Orange Free State in South Africa and completed an honor's degree in botany; later I also completed a master's degree in fisheries biology in Norway.

I started hunting professionally twelve years ago. This came to be after a biology study trip to Europe resulted in friends and lecturers from Norway wanting to visit Namibia for hunting. I took them out on an ad hoc basis, but found this to be more satisfying than my actual job. So I switched careers.

Currently I hunt all the general plains-game species, and also elephant, buffalo, lion, leopard, and other members of the dangerous-game group.

I am married to Rentia, who hails from the Kalahari, and we have two boys, Junior and Nicky, who love the outdoors and hunting.

Meet the Guides

Gerrit Utz
African Safari Trails
www.african-safari-trails.com
info@african-safari-trails.com

I started in 1989 by getting my certification as a hunting guide. In 1993, I obtained my status as a professional hunter, and in 1995 I finished the certification to become a big-game professional hunter. In 1998, I completed the certification for bow hunting guide, too.

My parents had a farm northeast of Windhoek where I grew up. My father started guiding in the early 1980s on his property, and when I was out of school during holidays and weekends, I helped with the hunts, working as a tracker. Soon, I was consumed with the idea of becoming a professional hunter.

I hunt more or less all of the plains-game species available in Namibia, but on my concession in Damaraland I also hunt elephant, lion, and leopard. Occasionally I hunt in the Caprivi for buffalo, hippo, and crocodile. Most of the hunting I do on my own property, which was formerly my parents' farm, and on my two Damaraland concessions.

Over the last few years I have specialized in sable, roan, waterbuck, and black-faced impala hunts on the farm, together with the other plains-game species of which we normally get good to very good trophies. Additionally, I enjoy the challenge of leopard hunts. In Damaraland, we have very good springbok and kudu hunts. In the last few years, we have been getting more hyenas in the area, and we were able to get some very big hyena trophies. Leopard and lion hunting is also excellent in this area.

Ask the Namibian Guides

John Wambach
Pro-Guiding Namibia
www.pro-guiding.biz
proguide@iway.na

I grew up in Zimbabwe on a cattle farm in the Zambezi Valley, where I started hunting for big game with my father and uncle at the age of eight. I have a bachelor's degree in psychology and a postgraduate degree in education; I also spent four years in the military, mostly in special forces units in southern Africa.

I have eighteen years of professional hunting experience. I served my apprenticeship controlling marauding lions, elephants, buffaloes, and hippos around Kruger National Park. For the past sixteen years, I have specialized in big-game safaris in South Africa, Zimbabwe, Mozambique, and Namibia. In addition, I have traveled and hunted extensively around the world, going on hunts in Europe, Argentina, and the United States and getting firsthand experience of what clients expect on an outfitted hunt.

I am extremely knowledgeable about all the animals, birds, insects, and plants in the areas we hunt, as well as the constellations seen in the crystal-clear African nights. I am a qualified pilot, hold professional big-game hunting licenses in three countries, and am a member of several professional hunting associations, including Safari Club International.

I have hunted the Big Five extensively and specialize in leopard, buffalo, and elephant. I also hunt all the southern African plains-game species, especially mountain zebra, kudu, klipspringer, oryx, and springbok. We operate concessions in the Salambala Conservancy, Kwando-Linyanti Conservancies, Buffalo Core area (Babwatha National Park), and Sanitatas-Orupembe-Marienfluss Conservancies (Kaokoland). We are one of the few safari operators offering backpack hunts for mountain species in Africa, including plains game and leopard.

Why Namibia?

Chapter 3

 Why should hunters choose Namibia for a safari rather than another place in Africa?

Janneman Brand: With its political and economic stability, good infrastructure, large ranches, abundance and variety of game, and the warm hospitality of our Namibian people, Namibia is the choice destination for the discerning hunter.

Dirk de Bod: Namibia is now the safest country in Africa, and has one of the largest selections of plains game as well as all the dangerous game. The

Exploring the deserts and scenic areas of this beautiful country is easy to do before or after a safari. (Photo courtesy of Dirk de Bod)

Ask the Namibian Guides

The Damara dik-dik is found only in Namibia. (Photo courtesy of Dirk de Bod)

country has very good infrastructure, roads, communication, modern hospitals and doctors, and nearly everyone speaks English. At nearly twice the size of Texas and with only two million people, Namibia has a lot of open space.

Kai-Uwe Denker: I do not necessarily think that hunters should choose Namibia rather than another place in Africa. Africa, with its various landscapes, is a fantastic continent to visit; it is the mecca for hunters. Any real hunter, gripped by the love of the African wilds, will naturally want to visit totally different African countries and habitats to experience the different game species in their natural and typical haunts. He perhaps will want to hunt the sable in the *miombo* woodland zone of Zimbabwe, Mozambique, Tanzania, and Zambia; the nyala in the dense low-lying brush of Zululand and Mozambique; and the waterbuck in the Zambezi Valley or the *bakos* of the Central African Republic.

But any discerning trophy hunter has to see Namibia as well, has to experience its harsh beauty and silent grandeur, has to hunt the greater kudu, the

Why Namibia?

gemsbok, and the springbok in their natural, most characteristic surrounding, which is the southwest arid zone of Africa.

I have traveled far and wide on the African continent, and I have hunted in the tropical rain forest and in the northwestern savanna, in Masailand and the Great Rift Valley, and along the Zambezi, Kwando, and Okavango Rivers. But still I consider the dry reaches of northwestern Namibia and the Namib Desert amongst the most spectacular on the continent.

I would advise any beginner not to do an "all-in-one" safari in Namibia or South Africa but to start off slowly with a plains-game safari (no kudu—this would be for the experienced connoisseur) in central Namibia, then return for a kudu and another specialty like Hartmann zebra in the escarpment. This will help the beginner thus acquire a taste and a feel for Africa.

And I would advise even the most experienced Africa hunter to also visit the true wilderness regions of Namibia. There are many great places to see in Africa, but there is no more spectacular country than Namibia.

Peter Kibble: First and foremost, it is a safe country and the people are friendly. There are no problems with bringing in firearms. The scenery is magnificent and so different as you travel from north to south and east to west. One can choose from an abundance of species to hunt, all with quality trophies.

Johan Kotzé: The biggest factors, I would say, are the size of the hunting areas and the variety of the animals in these areas. In a week's time, you could easily be able to hunt ten to fifteen different species in a given area. Most of these species are supported by their own breeding herds.

Corne Kruger: Namibia has an incredible variety of landscapes and different vegetation zones. The open spaces of Namibia and the beautiful night skies are two of our greatest assets. In addition, Namibia is a very easy country to travel to with firearms, and it has a hunting-friendly attitude.

Joof Lamprecht: The country of Namibia is a celebration of all that is wonderful about the magnificent continent of Africa! Namibia was named Deutsches Südwestafrika during German colonial rule, and then South-West Africa during the British and South African eras. Those who opposed colonial rule preferred the word Namibia. This word comes from a Nama/Damara word meaning *shield*, which is what the coastal desert, the Namib, did—it long protected the interior from access by sea.

As a people, we are proud of our young national identity; we have been a free and independent nation for seventeen years, and we take our fledgling democracy seriously.

Ask the Namibian Guides

The mountain zebra, one of Namibia's indigenous species, has a beautiful hide without the "shadow stripes" of the Burchell zebra. (Photo courtesy of Dirk de Bod)

About 1.8 million people share the vast spaces of Namibia, giving us one of the lowest population densities in the world with 1.5 people per square kilometer. Our population can be divided into at least eleven ethnic groups. Although our official language is English, Namibians speak nine different tongues, including some of the Khoisan languages, which include the "clicks" that are an enigma to most native English-speakers.

Each one of the country's cultural groups has its own rich heritage and traditions. However, due to the unfortunate apartheid history of Namibia (during South African rule), the division of people into cultural or tribal groups became an extremely sensitive issue, and we prefer to think of ourselves as Namibians.

Namibia offers hospitable, peace-loving people; political stability; international-standard private physicians and clinics; a well-developed and maintained road and telecommunication infrastructure; low population density and almost unlimited space; a safe, secure, and welcoming environment; something for every taste, from the sophisticated to the adventurous; world-

Why Namibia?

class standards in accommodation and services at affordable rates; almost 365 days of sunshine, endless blue skies, and much more.

This vast and pristine land is a haven for wildlife, nature, and cultures that are the embodiment of Africa, and yet unique in many ways. From the red undulating dunes of the Kalahari in the southeast to the desert-adapted elephants and black rhinos of the northwest, from the shifting sand dunes of the Namib and the desolate and lonely coastline to the celebration of life that is Etosha, and from the ancient San to the colorful Herero and their nomadic cousins, the Himba, Namibia is surely one of the most fascinating countries on earth.

Willem Mans: Choose Namibia for its tranquility, its vastness, its small population, its safety, and its abundance of wildlife—all types of flora and fauna.

Diethelm Metzger: Namibia is one of the most sparsely populated countries in Africa. Large areas have been left in their natural state with free-ranging game everywhere. Even in the ranching areas where fences have been built, game still roams freely, either jumping over the fence or crawling underneath. This gives the hunter and visitor a feeling of pristine wilderness that one will hardly find in other places.

Namibia is a healthy compromise between what one is used to from home, on the one hand, and wildest Africa on the other. Visitors can enjoy all the amenities such as taking a hot shower in the evening, sipping a nice red wine while sitting at the campfire watching millions of stars, and settling into a chalet for a good night's rest after a wholesome home-cooked meal. All these can be enjoyed while still being in deepest Africa the next morning and hunting for the magnificent kudu in the endless mountains of this semidesert country.

Namibia is characterized by its dual economy. On the one hand, there is the modern sector with modern hospitals and sophisticated banking, while on the other hand is the very rural sector with its subsistence farms. The country is known for its economic and political stability.

Peter Thormählen: Namibia is a beautiful and safe country, with a population of only around two million people. Its beauty lies in its huge, open spaces of unspoiled nature.

Jamy Traut: Choose Namibia for its scenery, political stability, big hunting areas, and generally unrestricted game movement that is the key to quality hunting.

Gerrit Utz: Our country is different from other frequently visited southern African countries. We have a much drier climate, and because of that the species of wildlife here are different. And the spectrum of hunting possibilities has everything possible, ranging from ranch hunting where, next to the game, cattle and sheep are bred; to hunting on ranches, fenced or unfenced, that hold only game; to communal conservancies run by the local people for plains game and dangerous game; to the government concessions, often in game reserves and parks.

Namibia has a history of good and fairly balanced legislation that supports hunting, and, in general, Namibia is a very hunter-friendly country. This friendliness starts at the airport, as it is easy (and cheap) to import your own rifles and ammunition. The rules are straightforward; every PH should know what to do and can inform the visiting hunter.

John Wambach: Namibia is definitely one of the safest and most developed countries in Africa for a hunter to visit. It has a wide range of options for the visiting hunter, from free-range hunting without fences in communal areas for both plains game and big game, to private game ranches catering to the individual who prefers all his game in one place and the luxury of staying in a lodge.

The infrastructure for trophy care and preparation is very good here, and seldom do hunters encounter problems with getting their trophies home in good condition. Namibia is also a good choice for hunting clients who bring a nonhunting partner along, in the sense that there are uncountable options for sightseeing and activities to keep them busy and happy.

 If money were of no object to a hunting client, what would be your idea of the perfect safari in Namibia?

Janneman Brand: Do a ten-day, plains-game safari, followed by a buffalo and elephant hunt in one of the northern concessions of Namibia.

Dirk de Bod: Hunt the game of the high plains, which include sable, roan, kudu, gemsbok, eland, waterbuck, lechwe, nyala, impala, springbok, klipspringer, Damara dik-dik, and Hartmann mountain zebra, with leopard.

Kai-Uwe Denker: The perfect safari in Namibia is not necessarily money-related. For very reasonable prices, one can conduct a safari for kudu, springbok, and Hartmann zebra at the edge of the Namib Desert or in the northwestern communal areas, which may turn out to be of such fascinating flair, with scenery and impressions of such overpowering grandeur, that for the rest of even an experienced hunter's life it will rank amongst the all-time greatest safaris.

Facilities—and views—like these are what make many Namibian safaris great getaways for the entire family. (Photo courtesy of Joof Lamprecht)

Of course there are high-priced, classic safaris for big game to be found as well. Some of the finest elephant safaris in Africa are conducted in some areas of northeastern Namibia. Here one can also hunt roan, sable, buffalo, kudu, springbok, and many other species.

Peter Kibble: A hunt for a number of species of big game, such as elephant and buffalo, followed by a hunt for plains game. Be sure to take enough time while doing this to explore and enjoy the countryside and the people.

Johan Kotzé: I hunted with a client from the United States once, and his six-year-old son was with him. His dad told him he could shoot a kudu on the safari. After he shot the kudu, I asked him what would be the next animal he would like to shoot if he had the opportunity. He replied, "We can start at the top of the list and work down from there!"

Corne Kruger: A plains game/leopard hunt combination in the northwestern conservancy areas of Namibia.

Choose from deluxe accommodations like these at Hunters Namibia Safaris, or rough it on a challenging backpack hunt—Namibia offers just about every type of safari experience. (Photo courtesy of Joof Lamprecht)

Joof Lamprecht: With a staggering list of huntable species in Namibia, one could book a 120-day safari and maybe not be able to collect them all. A hunter could combine hunting springbok and oryx in the spectacular Kalahari; elephant and hippo in the tropical, water-rich Caprivi; and rhinoceros and Hartmann zebra in breathtaking Damaraland.

Willem Mans: A fourteen-day plains-game and leopard hunt in southern Namibia, followed by a fourteen-day hunt for the other four members of the Big Five in the Caprivi Strip in the north.

Diethelm Metzger: If money were no issue, I would recommend a twenty-eight-day safari through Namibia. Start at Makadi Safaris, because we are situated only an hour's drive from the international airport, for a seven-day plains-game hunt. Trophies would include springbok, hartebeest, black and blue wildebeest, warthog, Burchell zebra, steenbok, and possibly duiker. Then, move on to the northeastern parts of the country for a four-day eland and waterbuck hunt. For some extra excitement and adrenaline rush, I would continue with a seven-day buffalo hunt in the Caprivi. During this hunt, other animals such as

Why Namibia?

reedbuck, roan, sable, and impala could also be taken. As money is no object, we could add some more days and also hunt for elephant.

Now, with travel time, we are already at day twenty. It is time to go back to the northwestern part of Namibia to hunt for Damara dik-dik. The safari will climax at Ilala Private Game Reserve, a property just recently acquired by Makadi Safaris. It is situated close to the Namib Desert. Ilala consists of a very mountainous area where we will hunt for mountain zebra, kudu, gemsbok, and klipspringer. We could also hunt for leopard here at Ilala. The object of this proposed hunt would not only be to hunt the different game species, but also to see and experience the different facets and areas of Namibia. With such a safari, one would get a very good feeling for Namibia and its people.

Peter Thormählen: I would recommend a twenty-eight-day safari for desert leopard, desert lion, and desert black rhino (subspecies *bicornis bicornis*). The unbelievable beauty of the Kaokoland/Damaraland region and the superior hunt for these members of the Big Five make for the perfect romantic African tented camp safari in the style of the old days.

Namibia is a top destination for springbok, which are plentiful and grow impressively long horns. (Photo courtesy of Peter Thormählen)

Unexpected experiences are part of the fun of travel. On her first trip to Namibia, the author never dreamed she'd get the chance to hold a lion cub! (Photo by J. Scott Rupp)

Why Namibia?

Jamy Traut: Spend at least a month camping under great camelthorn trees in an old-style safari. Your primary species would be elephant, but eland would occasionally make you stray from the big tracks. There would be no need to be out shooting something every day. In fact, numbers would not be important at all, and trophies would be admired but not measured. You would be tired in the evenings, but enjoy it with true friends around the fire.

Gerrit Utz: I would suggest a hunt of three to four weeks, hunting in two different areas of the county. Start with about a week of ranch hunting for species like roan, sable, tsessebe, eland, and waterbuck—species that are not available in the concession.

Then change hunting areas for the concession where the base is a comfortable tented camp. Spend fourteen to twenty days hunting in the concession for species such as lion and/or leopard and/or elephant. Combine this with plains-game hunting for trophies such as Damaraland springbok, greater kudu, klipspringer, gemsbok, Hartmann zebra, etc.

John Wambach: A twenty-one-day Big Five hunt that includes a black rhino, with sable and roan on the bag list as well.

And the opposite question—what sort of safari would you recommend to a hunter who is on a budget?

Janneman Brand: Depending on the size of the budget, I would suggest a seven-day safari package that includes three or four plains-game animals.

Dirk de Bod: A general plains-game hunt for kudu, gemsbok, hartebeest, blue wildebeest, impala, springbok, duiker, and steenbok.

Kai-Uwe Denker: For a hunter on a budget I would recommend a safari on an open farm in the central highlands. In general, for relatively little money, one can experience hospitality, tranquility, simplicity of life, and excellent hunting in the African veld for species like kudu, gemsbok, warthog, hartebeest, and others.

Peter Kibble: One can arrange to hunt a few plains-game animals by working with an outfitter to make up a suitable and affordable package.

Johan Kotzé: Most first-time hunts include kudu, oryx, springbok, warthog, and hartebeest. These animals are all very common throughout Namibia, and they all make good trophies.

Namibia is home to all of the Big Five, and is one of only two countries with a limited, legal hunt for black rhino. Money from these hunts is instrumental in the conservation of these rare animals. (Photo courtesy of Peter Thormählen)

Corne Kruger: Most Namibian hunting companies have great plains-game package hunts that include a set number of species for a predetermined price. These hunts are normally a great value for the money.

Joof Lamprecht: Affordable hunting is available on ranch hunts on private land. Almost all Namibian properties are large tracts of land with good populations of game present. Accommodations range from hunting lodges to guest rooms at the owner's house. All of the above is graded by the Namibian Tourism Board and must comply with stringent standards laid down by the Ministry of Tourism and Environment.

Willem Mans: I would suggest an eight-day plains-game hunt.

Diethelm Metzger: If you are on a budget, I would suggest a seven-day package hunt with gemsbok, hartebeest, springbok, warthog, and jackal included. No surprises—you pay once and get it all!

Why Namibia?

Even cheaper would be a management hunt. For the one-off price, one would be able to hunt for seven days for ten nontrophy animals.

Peter Thormählen: A seven-day hunt for plains game that includes gemsbok, springbok, kudu, impala, red hartebeest, blue wildebeest, and blesbok.

Jamy Traut: A general plains-game hunt, where eland takes the place of elephant, and you would track them daily. Kudu and gemsbok are musts, and so is mountain zebra. You can have an affordable and enjoyable time today hunting on cattle ranches in Namibia where game is still plentiful.

Gerrit Utz: A five- to seven-day hunt built on a tailor-made package with about four to five animals to hunt, such as kudu, hartebeest, gemsbok, blue or black wildebeest, zebra, warthog, and springbok. After the hunt, if still possible from the budget side, plan a few days to take a trip through the country to see some of the tourist attractions.

John Wambach: A ten-day hunt for six plains-game species will give the hunter a full experience and a full bag of trophies. Taking ten days will give him time to enjoy the hunt without having to rush, and maybe have a day or two of sightseeing as well. Species would be kudu, gemsbok, mountain zebra, red hartebeest, springbok, and warthog.

Is there any type of hunt in Namibia that you would tell hunters to avoid?

Janneman Brand: Any hunt that is not legal; make sure the outfitter you hunt with is reputable and follows the law.

Dirk de Bod: Ranch hunts where domestic animal farming is going on, and where there are a lot of interior fences and limited species.

Kai-Uwe Denker: I was born in Namibia and I love my home country with its unique, incomparable scenery. I feel that anyone visiting Namibia should experience and cherish the country in its typical and characteristic way. I would advise hunters to avoid "supermarket" hunts with guaranteed success and a dozen or more species offered. Species like nyala, waterbuck, lechwe, etc., are totally out of place in arid Namibia, and they should be hunted in their natural environment. One should not reduce a hunting experience to a trophy on the wall, but rather travel and hunt to experience unique and different settings.

Peter Kibble: Be wary of hunts that are very low cost. Avoid outfitters who cannot supply you with a number of credible references, and those who are

Ask the Namibian Guides

Joof Lamprecht and a client with a black-faced impala, a species found only in Namibia. (Photo courtesy of Joof Lamprecht)

not members of a reputable hunting organization (i.e., the Namibia Professional Hunting Association).

Johan Kotzé: Today, with the Internet, it is very easy to get information. Find out a bit about the outfitter you are interested in hunting with. You will quickly find out which outfitters have a good reputation in Namibia. Be careful if you find a cheap hunt—it might become pretty expensive at the end!

Corne Kruger: Like most countries, Namibia has some bad apples. Make sure before you book a hunt that you carefully check out an outfitter's reputation.

Joof Lamprecht: Any hunt offered by a nonresident of Namibia should be scrutinized carefully as some of these operators are working illegally and do not have the interests of Namibia at heart. A further recommendation is to book your safari with a registered member of the Namibia Professional Hunting Association.

Willem Mans: None that I know.

Why Namibia?

Diethelm Metzger: Avoid hunts where you are just a number, meaning that the outfitter takes too many hunters during a given year. Try to avoid those hunts where all hunting is conducted from the vehicle, driving around all day long—these are very boring and not very ethical! Beware: cheapest is not best.

Peter Thormählen: Yes, I'd say the cattle-farm safari where clients stay in the farmer's house and hunt in between his farming activities!

Jamy Traut: I would certainly ask for references about an area and an outfitter. If there are enough positive signs, I think you are good to go. Some regions may be hard to hunt in during the rainy season, so check with your outfitter or PH.

Gerrit Utz: Avoid outfitters that advertise or tell you that they can offer you a "guaranteed cat hunt" or have a "100-percent success rate" on any game animal. Nobody who is really hunting ethically and honestly can be sure to get a certain trophy; sometimes you only find youngsters, or the weather gives you a bad hand. And even on very common species, you can be unlucky.

Every PH offering cat hunts has had unsuccessful hunts. I am sure in the future I will have leopard or lion hunts that end without success, but I do everything possible to try to make each hunt successful.

John Wambach: None, but be very careful with whom you book a leopard hunt. It is imperative for a client to make sure if he is hunting dangerous game that he hunts with a big-game qualified PH who has experience with these animals.

 ## Are there particular animals in Namibia that are not found anywhere else in Africa, or are of better trophy quality here?

Janneman Brand: Mountain zebra, Damara dik-dik, black-faced impala (which cannot be exported to the United States), and black rhino. On average, Namibian trophies are of very high quality due to the good vegetation here and the large ranches.

Dirk de Bod: Hartmann mountain zebra, Damara dik-dik, and black-faced impala are found nowhere else in Africa, and we are the only country in the world that has cheetah on CITES quota.

Paintings of animals thought to have been made in ancient times by Bushmen are found on rocks in many areas.

Kai-Uwe Denker: The Namibian escarpment and adjacent areas are home to three endemic game species, namely Hartmann zebra, black-faced impala, and Damara dik-dik.

Namibia is well known as the greater kudu country, par excellence. Gemsbok and springbok of absolutely outstanding trophy quality amid matchless sceneries are to be found in the west and northwest, and the best Cape hartebeest trophies are to be found in eastern Namibia. And, of course, outstanding elephant trophies are taken regularly in the northeast.

Peter Kibble: Hartmann mountain zebra are endemic to Namibia; they are very challenging to hunt as they are very wary and live in tough terrain. Red hartebeest are also endemic, with many world-record-class animals taken here. They are also a challenge, as they seem to have eyes in the back of their heads!

We have the Damara dik-dik, which is also endemic and occurs only in Namibia. This country is noted for its magnificent southern greater kudu, gemsbok (oryx), and springbok.

Johan Kotzé: The Hartmann zebra and the black-faced impala. With the big gene pool that supports Namibia's hunting industry, the quality of all trophies is very good. We also have a minimum standard for all trophies that are exported out of the country, so every hunter can be sure that his or her trophies are of good value.

Corne Kruger: The Hartmann zebra, Damara dik-dik, and black-faced impala can only be hunted in Namibia. The springbok and gemsbok found in Namibia are the best in the world.

Joof Lamprecht: Endemic huntable species in Namibia are: Damara dik-dik, Angola or black-faced impala, and Hartmann zebra. Namibia is known for its great kudu, oryx, springbok, red hartebeest, roan, and sable. Outstanding buffalo and elephant trophies are recorded on a regular basis.

Willem Mans: The Hartmann mountain zebra is unique to Namibia and gemsbok, springbok, red hartebeest, and Cape eland seem to do better here than anywhere else.

Diethelm Metzger: The Hartmann zebra and the Damara dik-dik are unique to Namibia. The red hartebeest is originally from Namibia, and we have very good trophy quality here. The klipspringer, though not unique to Namibia, occurs here with very good trophy quality. The hunt for gemsbok and springbok in the desert is unique, and the trophy quality is very good.

Peter Thormählen: Animals that cannot be hunted anywhere else are the Damara dik-dik, black-faced impala, cheetah, desert elephant, and desert lion. Namibia boasts exceptionally good trophy quality for leopard, gemsbok, springbok, and lion.

Jamy Traut: The Hartmann mountain zebra and black-faced impala can only be hunted in Namibia, although they also occur in Angola in dubious numbers. Northeastern Namibia is home to impressive numbers of free-roaming eland, resulting in wonderful trophy quality. The same can be said for gemsbok and springbok in the Kalahari and in Damaraland (especially springbok). Everybody is aware of the world-class elephant bulls that are being taken in East Bushmanland—they are on par with the best elephants the rest of Africa has to offer.

Gerrit Utz: Animals not found anywhere else are black-faced impala, Damara dik-dik, and free-roaming Hartmann zebra. Cheetah can be hunted, but importation is not allowed for U.S. citizens. The same is true for black-faced impala.

Trophy quality is generally better on Kalahari springbok, red hartebeest, and southern roan in Namibia than it is in our neighboring countries.

Namibia is known for producing some huge elephants, like this bull with 90-pound tusks taken with elephant-hunting specialist Kai-Uwe Denker. (Photo courtesy of Kai-Uwe Denker)

Why Namibia?

John Wambach: Mountain zebra, black-faced impala, and Damara dik-dik. The kudu, springbok, gemsbok, and red hartebeest trophies in Namibia are the best in the world.

 Are there any safety issues hunters should be aware of when booking a safari in Namibia?

Janneman Brand: Ask your outfitter what health precautions are required for his hunting area (e.g., malaria prophylaxis). The U.S. Health Department will also advise on safety requirements for Namibia. Namibia is considered one of the safest African countries. In city areas, though, watch your cameras and purses.

Dirk de Bod: No, not at all. Namibia is the safest country in Africa.

Kai-Uwe Denker: No, none.

Peter Kibble: If going north, one must take prophylaxis for malaria. Central Namibia and the coast, however, are free of malaria. Just as in any country, be aware of your valuables and do not flaunt cash around; just carry a small amount. It's best to insure yourself and your property. Crime is very low in Namibia compared to other countries in Africa and around the world.

Johan Kotzé: Other than malaria, which is only found in the far northern reaches of the country, there aren't any. Namibia has a very good reputation of being one of the safest countries in Africa.

Corne Kruger: There are none.

Joof Lamprecht: Namibia is an extremely safe and healthy environment, and there are no health or safety issues. The great roads, infrastructure, accommodations, and gas stations make traveling easy, pleasant, and safe.

Willem Mans: Not that I know of. Southern Namibia is probably the safest place on earth—you can still sleep under the stars or with wide-open doors and windows.

Diethelm Metzger: Nothing, really. Namibia is a very safe country. The rural areas, especially, have hardly any crime. Should one visit one of the local markets, the outfitter will probably explain the do's and don'ts.

Peter Thormählen: No. Namibia is a very safe country.

Jamy Traut: There is some petty crime in the cities.

Gerrit Utz: There is a higher crime rate in the larger cities than elsewhere in the country, but common sense should prevail.

John Wambach: There are no safety issues that are of any importance to visiting hunters.

 If your visiting hunter wanted to visit a scenic area or do something other than hunt while in the country, what would you recommend?

Janneman Brand: I would suggest visiting Etosha National Park, the Caprivi Strip, Swakopmund and the Namib Desert, Naukluft, and Sesriem. We assist clients with all arrangements for side trips in Namibia.

Dirk de Bod: Etosha National Park, Okavango River lodges, Caprivi, Zambezi river lodges, Skeleton Coast, Namib Desert, Swakopmund, and Fish River Canyon. I'd also suggest fishing in the Okavango and Zambezi for tigerfish and predator bream, tilapia, and giant catfish. I'd also suggest fishing along the Skeleton Coast, both offshore and in the surf, for sharks and other species.

Kai-Uwe Denker: I would recommend visiting Etosha National Park, Fish River Canyon, and Sossusvlei. These are, perhaps, the most stunning places, but there is such a wealth of interesting places that I could not name them all.

Peter Kibble: Go on a photographic tour to Etosha or one of the other national parks. Go fishing, either at the coast or on the Kavango River. Either one will allow you to see the countryside. There is also plenty of shopping. Windhoek is a very cosmopolitan town and also has many curio shops. Many stones are mined in Namibia and made into beautiful jewelry, which is sold at very reasonable prices to the overseas customer.

Johan Kotzé: The variety is endless. We have the second-biggest canyon in the world, after the Grand Canyon. It's called Fish River Canyon. In the Namib Desert, we have the biggest dunes in the world. The Skeleton Coast is a very big attraction, with its shipwrecks and seal colonies. To the north, there are beautiful areas like Damaraland and Kaokoland that are still untouched; you will still find nomadic tribes living in these areas. Etosha National Park is a wonderful area to explore and a great place to see a lot of animals, including lions, elephants, and the rare black rhino. Then, up in the northeastern section of the country, in the Caprivi, there are beautiful rivers. All of these areas are easily reached with the good road network we have, and in all of these areas there are tourist lodges with high standards.

Why Namibia?

Namib Naukluft Park encompasses part of the Namib Desert and the scenic Naukluft mountain range.

Corne Kruger: There are too many to name! The destinations that come immediately to mind are Sossusvlei, Etosha National Park, Erindi Private Game Reserve, Swakopmund, and Kaokoland.

Joof Lamprecht: Namibia boasts remarkable natural attractions such as the Namib Desert, Skeleton Coast, Fish River Canyon, Kalahari Desert, Etosha National Park, and Caprivi Strip. Namibia's capital city, Windhoek, as well as the coastal town of Swakopmund, are highly recommended destinations during your Namibian adventure.

Known as the world's oldest desert, the Namib stretches almost 1,242 miles along the coast of Namibia, from the Orange River on the southern border with South Africa up north beyond the Kunene River into Angola, to form one of the most spectacular and richest deserts in the world. Gently sloping toward the Atlantic Ocean, it is patterned by a sea of giant red sand dunes, some which reach 1,000 feet high.

The Skeleton Coast, an evocative name for Namibia's hostile northern seaboard, was a graveyard for unwary ships whose surviving sailors over the centuries came ashore to die in the harsh wastes of the Namib Desert.

The breathtaking Fish River Canyon, situated in southern Namibia, is the second-largest canyon in the world after the Grand Canyon in the United States.

This area is noted for its remarkable geological features with rock strata of grays, purples, and pinks formed over hundreds of millions of years.

The immense Kalahari Desert spans South Africa, Botswana, and Namibia. Although it is referred to as a desert, the landscape is surprisingly well vegetated, and in springtime the undulating, red sandy plains are covered in carpets of flowers and green grass. It is a region of great beauty and infinite vastness. The Kalahari is home to some of the best springbok and gemsbok trophies in the world.

Etosha National Park is one of southern Africa's largest and finest game parks, and covers an area of 13,837 square miles. Etosha, meaning *Great White*

PH Gerrit Utz and hunter Herb Rudolf handled this problem lion in Damaraland in 2008. (Photo courtesy of Gerrit Utz)

Why Namibia?

Place, is home to 114 mammal species, 340 bird species, 110 reptile species, and 16 amphibian species.

The Caprivi Strip is a long panhandle enclosed by the permanent waters of the Kwando, Linyanti, Chobe, and Zambezi Rivers. The Caprivi stretches eastward, ending at the border junction of Namibia, Botswana, Zimbabwe, and Zambia. This area offers an ecologically diverse combination of grassland, woodland, flood plain, riverine forests, and reedbeds, supporting more than 60 mammal and nearly 350 bird species.

Our capital, Windhoek, lies in the heart of the central highlands and is surrounded by mountains. This is one of the safest, cleanest, and best organized capital cities in Africa. Windhoek is a truly cosmopolitan city that offers a variety of excellent dining options as well as great shopping for locally manufactured crafts, jewelry, leather, locally embroidered linen, and more.

Swakopmund, our country's second biggest town and Namibia's most popular holiday destination, is a charming seaside resort nestled in the mist on the Atlantic shore between the dunes of the Namib Desert and the intriguing Skeleton Coast, and is the ideal location from which to explore these fascinating areas.

Willem Mans: Sossusvlei, which features the highest dunes in the world, is a must. A self-drive tour along the Atlantic Coast can be very rewarding.

Diethelm Metzger: Depending on where the hunt was conducted I would suggest the following:

Day 1: Leave Makadi for Etosha National Park, which is about a six-hour drive. At Etosha one can observe big game in its natural surroundings.

Day 2–3: Spend two days at Etosha and enjoy the wildlife.

Day 4: Travel to any of the lodges to the west of Etosha, called Damaraland. Experience the scenery.

Day 5: Travel to Swakopmund, an old colonial-style town built where the desert reaches the Atlantic Ocean.

Day 6: Spend the day in Swakopmund shopping, sightseeing, or quad biking in the dunes, or take a dolphin cruise, fish, or take a desert trip to see the oldest plant, the welwitschia.

Day 7: Travel to Ilala Private Game reserve, a three-hour drive.

Day 8: Let the enormous landscape make an impression on you. Enjoy the Bushman paintings, go swimming in the pool, or explore the family library.
Day 9: Back to Makadi or the airport, or spend half a day shopping in Windhoek.

Peter Thormählen: I would recommend the west coast town of Swakopmund, Etosha National Park, the Namib Desert, Kaokoland, and Damaraland.

Jamy Traut: Namibia has places of great interest all over. Depending on where you hunt, you could, for example, see Fish River Canyon or experience the diamond areas in the Namib Desert when you are hunting in the south. See Etosha and Damaraland when you are in the north, and Khaudum Game Reserve and the Caprivi wetlands if you want to spend a few more hours driving northeast. The surf fishing on the west coast is great, and so is the fishing in the northeastern wetlands. Make sure you allow enough time to explore when you are visiting Namibia.

Gerrit Utz: I definitely recommend a visit to Etosha National Park, and tours of Vingerklip and Twyfelfontein in Damaraland can be combined. Swakopmund and the Namib Desert are also worth the trip. If you have a lot of time, a tour of the Caprivi Strip is also a must.

John Wambach: I would definitely recommend the Namib Desert, the Skeleton Coast, and Etosha National Park.

Selecting a Safari Guide

Chapter 4

 How should a prospective safari hunter go about finding a Namibian outfitter?

Janneman Brand: I suggest visiting the various hunting conventions in the United States. This enables the hunter to meet different outfitters, view their portfolios, and personally ask questions. I strongly believe that choosing an outfitter is a very personal choice; you need to find the outfitter with whom you make a connection and with whom you will want to spend time in the African bush! Make sure to follow up on recommendations and references.

Dirk de Bod: First, get references from previous clients and ask them about the hunter and his operation, the size of the hunting area or game ranch, what species are available, and general information. Also find out how far you will have to travel for certain species if all the species you are looking for are not found in one location. Don't just go for the cheapest option. Remember, you get what you pay for, and there is always a reason why something is cheap.

Kai-Uwe Denker: The *Huntinamibia* magazine (www.venturepublications. com.na) offers a lot of information to start your search. Select a few suitable outfitters and get in contact with them. Come up with a list of questions that are relevant to you and strongly spell out issues that are important to you; for example, are you amenable to hunting where there are fences? Is hunting on foot an option for you? Are all the hunts fair chase? The questions are endless.

Peter Kibble: Make sure your outfitter is a professional hunter (not a hunting guide). He or she should have a certificate issued from the office of the Ministry of Wildlife and Tourism. If you are into fair-chase hunting, ask for references from other hunters who have hunted with the outfitter, and find out how the hunting was done; i.e., walking, stalking, and not shooting over water holes or off the vehicle.

Finally, make sure the outfitter has several years of experience guiding international hunting guests and that he can provide references.

Johan Kotzé: Visit hunting shows, do research on the Internet, and contact references. Most important, talk to hunters who have been to Namibia. I think

Some of the tusks taken by PH Kai-Uwe Denker in 2010. Success like this speaks for itself when you are researching an outfitter. (Photo courtesy of Kai-Uwe Denker)

word of mouth is where you get the true story. I always say that everybody can write good stories about their camps and their hunting operation, and everybody can take good pictures, but if you want the true story, talk to hunters who have been there.

Corne Kruger: First, decide what your needs are for the hunt. Always remember you cannot compare apples and pears when it comes to price! Decide how much you want to spend, and what animals you want to spend it on. Always talk to the references the outfitter provides. And make sure the outfitter knows what you expect of the hunt, so he can tell you if that is what you will experience.

Joof Lamprecht: A smart trophy hunter will first select the professional hunter he wants to hunt with and then start planning his safari around the species that his PH has available. By checking references with hunting clients who have hunted with the prospective PH, you'll be amazed as to what kind of information you'll hear. Your next step is to meet with your PH at the annual SCI Convention in Nevada or Dallas Safari Club Convention in Dallas. You should meet the man face to face and then decide whether you are willing to live with him for weeks at a time in some of the most remote and wildest parts of Africa.

Just a bit of friendly advice: When you meet him, if he carries multiple scars of attacks from various wild animals, stay away from him, unless you want to do "extreme hunting," become a Rambo, and stab your way out of the teeth, claws, and horns of various animals.

Now that you've met the guy, and you like what you see, do not, in heaven's name, ask him whether he can guarantee you those monster trophies that you've been dreaming about. My standard retort to a question like that is: "How much time do you have?" If the client is willing to book a six-month safari with me, he has got a very good chance of getting all those monster trophies and more. In the limited time frame of a weeklong safari, depending on your skill and luck, you will collect some dream trophies and some good, representative trophies.

Once you've booked with the PH, read through his literature carefully; most of your questions regarding clothing, caliber, temperatures, malaria prophylaxis, visas, etc., should be answered there. Don't draw up one of those long questionnaires, of which I have received too many. Read the literature again and make sure that your questions haven't already been answered.

Willem Mans: Try to meet the outfitter in person unless you have a very good reference from somebody you know who has hunted with that person before. Once you have met him, check his references anyway.

Diethelm Metzger: Establish contact by going to hunting shows and conventions or through other advertisements. Word of mouth also works very well. After having established contact, verify the information by either contacting people on the reference list or by contacting the local hunting association to find out more about the outfitter and his reputation. And remember: Special deals and cheap hunts are directly linked to the quality of a hunt.

Peter Thormählen: It depends on the client and the animals he is after. The best method is good old word-of-mouth references. Talk to hunters who have been there.

Visit the Dallas Safari Club and the Safari Club International conventions to seek out the superior outfitters. The hunting community is small; if you start asking around, you will soon run into the same names frequently. The Web is proving to be a successful way to find good outfitters, but combine your research with follow-up by phoning and e-mailing references.

Jamy Traut: Go to the NAPHA Web site and have a look at potential outfitters. Also, going to the SCI, DSC, and other hunting conventions makes a lot of sense as it allows you to get a feel for the personality of the various outfitters. Once you've narrowed down your choices, ask for references. Certain areas are likely to be better for certain species; try to match up your wish list to the area and the PH.

Gerrit Utz: The easiest way is through recommendations from friends who have hunted with an outfitter and were happy with what they received. Word of mouth is still the most reliable way to get good service.

The next step would be getting addresses out of magazines like *Huntinamibia,* finding the type of hunt you are looking for (in terms of species you are interested in, etc.), contacting the outfitters, and then making the effort to see these outfitters at a convention. The Internet also plays a big part in choosing an outfitter today. Many outfitters can be found at the annual hunting conventions in Europe and America. It is a good opportunity to meet and talk to people, and to find out if your hunting preferences match up to those of the outfitter.

John Wambach: Visiting the hunting shows is a good start, as you can meet your outfitter face to face and then visit the booth of the organization he belongs to and do a bit of research. Web sites are good sources, but references

Be sure to ask about the type of accommodation provided, whether it's a lodge or a safari tent in a scenic wilderness concession like this one. (Photo courtesy of Peter Kibble)

should always be checked. Find someone who has been to Namibia and ask his or her advice. And read *Sports Afield!*

 How can a prospective client know whether a particular PH/outfit is a good one for Namibia? For example, is there a particular type of license the PH should have, and should he belong to an organization?

Janneman Brand: Make sure you hunt with a qualified and registered Namibian professional hunter. When an outfitter is a member of the Namibian Professional Hunting Association, or NAPHA (our hunting organization in Namibia), the client has another point of reference. Follow-up on references, ask questions, and ask around.

Dirk de Bod: Clients should ensure that they are booked and will be hunting with a Namibia Tourism Board (NTB) registered trophy-hunting

PH Willem Mans and his wife, Marita, at their booth at a hunting convention in the USA. (Photo courtesy of Willem Mans)

operator, as well as a Ministry of Environment and Tourism (MET) registered Namibian hunting professional. The three classifications of hunting professionals are: hunting guide, master hunting guide, and professional hunter. Two specialist qualifications are: big-game professional hunter—a registered Namibian professional hunter who has passed the big-game examination; and bow-hunting professional hunter—a registered Namibian hunting professional with an additional bow-hunting qualification.

Kai-Uwe Denker: The good ones have a solid reputation, which can easily be assessed when inquiring with some more experienced hunters. Strongly consider giving a young, idealistic outfitter a chance, it may be very satisfactory and enjoyable. Just try to figure out whether he is truly idealistic or just one of the many show-business operators.

Peter Kibble: Make sure the outfitter is a member of a recognized hunting association in the country in which you are hunting. It's even better if he is a member of other professional hunting associations as well. Make sure that the outfitter has permits for all of the animals you intend to hunt before going hunting.

Johan Kotzé: Professional hunters must be registered with the Ministry of Environment and Tourism. Accommodations must be registered with the Namibia Tourism Board. Also, check with the Namibia Professional Hunting Association to find out if the PH is a member.

Corne Kruger: It does not always help that someone is a member of a particular organization, as sometimes the bad apples are members too. Research an outfitter's reputation, and go by that. A reputation does not lie.

Joof Lamprecht: Namibia has two categories of professional hunters. The plains-game professional hunter is called just that, but for dangerous game you need a qualification called big-game professional hunter. Preferably he should be a member of the Namibian Professional Hunting Association.

Willem Mans: The Namibian Professional Hunting Association (NAPHA) has a very proud and ethical code of conduct. If a PH is not a member of this organization, there may be something cooking—worse, he may not even be registered as a PH with the ministry, which is required for anyone to conduct legal trophy hunting.

Diethelm Metzger: All hunting professionals have to have a hunting license, which means that they have passed a test and have gained a few years of experience hunting and guiding trophy hunters. All PHs have to be registered with the registering authority, the Ministry of Environment and Tourism (MET). All outfitters have to be registered with the Namibian Tourism Board (NTB). Being a member of the Namibian Professional Hunting Association (NAPHA) is voluntary. All NAPHA members have to be registered with MET and NTB as a prerequisite. They have to sign a code of conduct and ethics, which should ensure a certain standard for the offered hunt.

Peter Thormählen: Good outfitters are well known. They are approved through years of being in business. It is a grueling, hard road for an outfitter to get to the point where he has a good reputation in the industry. I am amazed about the naivety of prospective clients—how they will book a big safari without checking any references because the outfitter has low prices. The only foolproof way to ensure a good hunt is still to get references and to call and ask questions and hear what these references have to say.

The license is irrelevant, in my opinion, as any outfitter registered at the Namibian Tourism Board (NTB) can legally sell any type of hunt. If, for example, it is a Big Five hunt, then he just contracts with a Namibian qualified Big Five PH for the duration of the hunt. So having a Big Five license in Namibia does not necessarily make you a reputable outfitter. It just allows you to guide a dangerous-game hunt legally in Namibia.

I do not believe that belonging to an organization, specifically a professional hunting association, is a guarantee that you are a reputable outfitter. I have met and done business with outstanding outfitters in both Namibia and South Africa who did not belong to a professional hunting organization, while the contrary is also true with outfitters that belong to their professional hunting association. The hunting organizations have no legal power; they are merely conveying an opinion.

Jamy Traut: If dangerous game is on your list, make sure your PH is registered for big game. Again, checking references and visiting the NAPHA Web site may be of great help. Although outfitters don't have to belong to NAPHA, it's a good idea to choose someone who is part of the organization.

Gerrit Utz: We have a professional hunters' association in Namibia (NAPHA), and most outfitters and professional hunters in the country are members. NAPHA tries to keep its standards and ethics as high as possible. If a person belonging to the organization does not adhere to the rules, that person is questioned. Asking NAPHA about a person or outfitter gives you a good idea about him. Being a member of NAPHA does not necessarily make him a "good" or reputable outfitter, but to stay in the organization you are obligated to follow the rules.

Word of mouth is still the best. Ask the outfitter for a list of references.

John Wambach: The Namibian hunting industry has a grading system for its hunters. It is important that the client finds out what his outfit/hunter is qualified to hunt. Hunting guides may hunt only plains game on one farm. Master hunting guides may only hunt plains game on two farms. Professional hunters may hunt only plains game (and leopard) in any areas where no big game is present. Big-game professional hunters may hunt all game in all areas.

The law allows hunting guides, master hunting guides, and professional hunters to hunt leopard, although they have had no training and have not been tested to qualify to hunt this dangerous animal. It is imperative for a client who wants to hunt dangerous game to make sure to hunt with a big-game qualified PH.

Annual hunting conventions like those sponsored by the Dallas Safari Club and Safari Club International are great places to meet and talk with outfitters you are interested in hunting with.

 ## What questions should a prospective client ask when booking a safari?

Janneman Brand: Ask for references. How many years of experience does the outfitter have? Who will be guiding you on your safari? Where will you be hunting? How far is the drive between the different concession areas? How much time will you be spending on the road (driving to different areas for different species), and how much time will you spend in the field? What species are available on each hunting concession? How many hunters will be in camp at one time? What is the price structure?

Dirk de Bod: Is he a guide, master guide, or PH? Will you hunt with him or someone else? Get references—this is very important. How big is the land

If leopard is on your wish list, be sure to choose a PH who is certified to hunt dangerous game. (Photo courtesy of Gerrit Utz)

he hunts on—is it a game ranch, game reserve, cattle/sheep ranch? What are the species available? How far will you have to travel to hunt various species? What are the accommodations like?

Kai-Uwe Denker: The prospective hunter should clearly spell out his preferences to the PH; he should also trust his gut feeling and check references. All outfitters—and especially the dubious ones—know how to answer any question in an evasive way if they want to do so.

Peter Kibble: Is the outfitter a member of a recognized hunting association in the country you are hunting, and does he have permits for all of the animals you intend to hunt?

Johan Kotzé: Find out everything about the costs involved in safari—what is included in the price and what is not included. Where will the hunt take place, and will there be a lot of driving to other concessions? Are all the animals to be hunted found on the property where the outfitter hunts, or are some species hunted in other places?

Corne Kruger: Make sure you know where, exactly, your hunt will be conducted and make sure the outfitter knows what you expect from the hunt.

Selecting a Safari Guide

Temperatures in different parts of Namibia can vary a lot; make sure you ask about this.

If you are hunting leopard, be sure to ask for a copy of your hunting permit and the tag as well. Make sure you actually see these documents.

Joof Lamprecht: Apart from the obvious questions like game species and area, ask who will be on the ground when you arrive and who will be your PH. You have to talk to your PH to see if you want to spend all that time with him alone in the bush. See if he's your type of person.

Willem Mans: Is your outfitter registered with a professional hunting body? Will there be a fair chance of getting the trophies on your wish list? Will there be other parties hunting at the same time, or is exclusivity guaranteed? Who will be the guide? (It's of no use to meet a nice, competent guy at a show and then hunt with a stranger.) What is included and not included in the daily rates? What are the circumstances and quality of the accommodations? What are the conditions of transfer to and from the airport?

Diethelm Metzger: Ask for a list of references. Then ask about the size of the property, whether it is fenced or not, the availability of game, the climate, what kind of accommodation is provided, how many hunters does the outfitter host each year, how many hunters are in camp at one time, and in what geographical area the hunt will take place.

Peter Thormählen: How many years have you been operating as an outfitter? (This is no guarantee, but at least it says that the outfitter has done something right if he has been in business for a long time.) What concessions are you hunting on? How large are they, where are they located, and what species are available?

Ask for a reference list of past clients. Ask to see photos of the accommodations and recent trophies. Ask for a list of professional hunters who will be guiding clients, with their photos. Also, does the operation have a Web site? If so, look at the photos of trophies, camps, and concessions.

Jamy Traut: I would ask about what method of hunting will be used for different species, how far will you be expected to walk, how fit you need to be, what type of shooting scenarios will you need to practice for, how cold or warm will it be, what type of rifle/caliber/ammunition should be used for the species in question, and what type of clothes and shoes should be worn.

Gerrit Utz: How big is the area where the client will be hunting? Is there a lot of driving to different concessions for certain animals, or are they all found on the same property/area? What kind of camp or lodge can be expected? Who will be guiding the hunt? Is it an open or closed area? Will there be other hunters in camp during the hunt?

John Wambach: What PH qualification does the hunter have? What is his experience and where has he hunted? Is the game free ranging or fenced? What are the accommodations like? What is the style of hunting (walking and stalking, driving and spotting, shooting from the truck, sitting in blinds at water holes, etc.)? How are trophy preparations and game care in camp handled? Can I get a list of references? Also, you should receive a contract for the hunt.

 ## What kind of person would be your ideal safari client?

Janneman Brand: Someone who has a passion for hunting and Africa, as well as someone who comes prepared to hunt in Africa.

Dirk de Bod: A true hunter who admires and respects the game and listens to the PH.

Kai-Uwe Denker: A true nature lover in good physical shape.

Peter Kibble: One who follows the instructions given to him, who is reasonably fit, and who is a reasonably good shot.

Johan Kotzé: Somebody who comes to enjoy nature and enjoy the hunt. It is the PH's job to find the client the best trophies.

Corne Kruger: A hunter who respects wildlife and hunting, and who knows how to have fun!

Joof Lamprecht: I am a conservationist first and a hunter second. My ideal client is a person who is willing to learn, and a person who respects the fauna and flora. He must be willing to go the extra mile and appreciate the beauty of Africa.

Willem Mans: Someone with good manners, a moderate lifestyle, and respect for nature in all its spheres.

Diethelm Metzger: A person who wants to have fun. Someone who enjoys and appreciates nature and hunting.

Peter Thormählen: A client who trusts his professional hunter! I have seen over the years that the clients who come on safari after they have done their homework on outfitter selection and who trust their PH to find the game they requested are the clients who harvest the best trophies.

Selecting a Safari Guide

The clients who are patient, well mannered, who do not complain or challenge the PH the whole time are the dream clients. They give the PH the freedom to work his butt off to get them good trophies. They give the PH the freedom to go to plan B or C or even Z to get the client outstanding trophies, as the PH does not have to spend frustrating time listening to complaints or demands. The worst clients are the ones who know more about professional hunting than the professionals do! I have harvested the most outstanding trophies with clients who were patient and well mannered.

Jamy Traut: Someone who really likes to be outdoors, who can appreciate the little things, and who is not focused only on the size of each trophy. A person who respects everybody else in camp, and his or her quarry as well. The hunter who is constantly walking around with a tape measure in hand lessens the experience for everybody, including himself.

Gerrit Utz: The ideal hunter is one who does not consider his hunting safari to be an "inch contest" and who does not get too anxious about success. It is someone who does not pressure everybody around him to make success happen, no matter how, but who also looks at his hunt as a fun experience. This is a person who takes the attitude of "Let's see what we can achieve." Those hunters generally are the "lucky" ones, bringing home most of the trophies they wanted and more. My team and I try everything possible to make a safari successful, whether we are pressured to do so or not.

John Wambach: Someone who is there for the real adventure of hunting, who knows that there are no guarantees, and who wants a real experience and not a watered-down, commercialized trip. Trophy size does not determine the quality of the hunt, but the chase does, and getting a representative head from an old, nonproductive animal is the ultimate memory to place on the wall and to remember a great hunt by.

Rifles and Gear for a Namibian Safari

Chapter 5

 What rifle caliber do you like to see clients carrying when hunting with you? (Address rifle and caliber choices for both plains game and dangerous game, if both are hunted in your area.)

Janneman Brand: For plains-game hunting, I recommend using the rifle you are most accustomed to. It is more about shot placement than the size of the bullet. Visit the NAPHA Web site (www.natron.net/napha) for minimum requirements. For all plains-game species smaller than eland, I would use a .30-caliber rifle with a good bonded bullet. For eland, I suggest a .338 Winchester Magnum.

Dirk de Bod: For plains game, a .300 Winchester Magnum or similar rifle with a good 6X scope is the best choice. You must be able to shoot it well off of shooting sticks from 50 to 200 yards. For small game, use a .223 with a good scope. For dangerous game, use a .375 H&H, .375 Ruger, .416 Rigby, or similar caliber with a 1.5–6X scope; you must be able to shoot it well off of sticks from 20 to 80 yards.

Kai-Uwe Denker: This is very much a standard. Any .300 caliber for plains game, and .375 or more for dangerous game.

Peter Kibble: For plains game, I like to see bolt-action rifles in .300 Winchester Magnum, .338 Winchester Magnum, or .375 H&H, with good scopes. For dangerous game, my choices would be the .375 H&H, .416 Rigby, .458 Winchester Magnum, or, for doubles, .470 Nitro Express or .500 Nitro Express.

It is important that none of these rifles have a Mag-Na-Port or any form of muzzle brake, as these are terribly dangerous to the hearing of the PH and trackers.

Johan Kotzé: African game is very tough. The .300 Winchester Magnum is a very popular caliber and will do the job on most animals. It is also good for long-distance shooting, and its ability to shoot heavier grain bullets makes it very effective. So any caliber in that range is perfect for plains game.

Most PHs recommend dark clothing that blends with the terrain, as well as comfortable boots for stalking. It pays off! (Photo courtesy of Dirk de Bod)

Corne Kruger: For plains game, I like to see hunters carry a .300 Winchester Magnum. For big game, my preference is the .458 Lott.

Joof Lamprecht: The rifle is one of the most important tools on a safari and if you take a piece of rubbish to Africa, it will turn into a disaster. In most countries, semiautomatic weapons are not allowed, so forget about them. The rifle the client carries must be one that he is comfortable with. The old saying, "use enough gun," is valid, providing the client can shoot it and is comfortable with it.

For lighter weight clients shooting plains game, I like a .300 Winchester Magnum. If a client can handle something a bit bigger, I recommend a .338 Winchester Magnum. I do not care much for the .375 H&H because of its ballistics. A .458 Winchester Magnum or, if the client can handle it, the .416 Rigby or .416 Winchester Magnum will serve him much better.

This is a large elephant for Damaraland, with tusks of 87 and 52 pounds, respectively. Big-bore doubles are a good choice for elephant, and solid bullets are the only way to go. (Photo courtesy of Gerrit Utz)

Willem Mans: Any caliber of .300 or higher is ample for both plains game and leopard.

Diethelm Metzger: The most important consideration in rifle choice is the kilojoules—the rifle must have enough kilojoules to kill the animals effectively. My second recommendation is that the hunter should bring a rifle that he is comfortable with—a rifle he knows and shoots well. For a plains-game hunt, the gun should be in the range of .270 to .336. The .300 calibers are very popular, and those are the rifles we see most. If the hunter considers bringing two rifles, one should be a smaller caliber (.243) for duiker, springbok, and steenbok. For the bigger plains game, he should bring a .300 caliber. If eland is on the hunter's wish list, he should consider a .338 or .375.

For dangerous game, the required calibers by law are .375 and up, although I would recommend .416 and up. Again, one should make sure of being comfortable with the rifle, even if it means spending quite some time at the shooting range before the hunt commences.

Peter Thormählen: For plains game, the .300 calibers have proven themselves over and over. For dangerous game, the .375 H&H or .416 are both very good choices as most clients are not as used to recoil as are those of us who shoot big guns often.

Rifles and Gear for a Namibian Safari

Jamy Traut: The client should use the rifle he or she shoots the best, shoots the most, and feels the most comfortable with. For plains game in bushveld conditions, where shots are, as a rule, shorter (80 to 130 yards), the old .30-06 or even the .308 Winchester is more than ample, as long as the hunter knows its limitations. In the Namibian mountains or in desert areas, the flatter-shooting .300 calibers (.300 Winchester Magnum, .300 Winchester Short Magnum), is an ideal choice. Whatever rifle is used, it should feed well and be accurate.

For big game, use the biggest caliber you feel comfortable with. I like it when a client shows up with a .416 Rigby or .416 Remington if his rifle is a bolt-action. If he uses a double, the .470 NE is a great choice. Although the .458 Winchester Magnum has taken some abuse, I find that most hunters are less intimidated by the recoil of this caliber, resulting in more consistent, accurate shooting. Modern ammo has done away with the problems with low muzzle velocities that plagued this caliber in the past.

If a hunter is going to shoot both plains game and dangerous game with one rifle, the .375 H&H is probably the number-one choice, but if he can handle the recoil, the .416 is great as well.

Gerrit Utz: My favorite caliber for Africa is the .375 H&H Magnum. I believe it is the best all-round caliber for a hunter coming to Africa. A hunter can shoot all the dangerous game safely with it (although it should not be used as a back-up rifle) and all the plains game from eland to steenbok. If you are hunting in dense brush for elephant or buffalo, bring a caliber around the .500 class, or if you hunt plains game and plan to take shots at long distances you should look at something in the .300 Winchester or .300 Weatherby range.

If you want to take just one rifle, my personal choice would be a bolt-action .375 H&H Magnum.

John Wambach: For plains game, any of the .30-calibers (.30-06, .300 Winchester Magnum, etc.) are adequate. For dangerous game, I prefer any caliber above .375, but I especially like the .458 Lott.

 ## What bullet types do you recommend?

Janneman Brand: I recommend any bonded bullet or the Barnes Triple-Shock X-Bullet.

Ask the Namibian Guides

Dirk de Bod: For plains game, 180-grain Barnes X-Bullet or Swift A-Frame. For dangerous game, Barnes X-Bullet or Swift A-Frame and solids.

Kai-Uwe Denker: Any hard, welded-core softnose bullet, and any FMJ with a strong jacket.

Peter Kibble: I recommend Swift A-Frame, Trophy Bonded Bear Claw, Norma Oryx, and Woodleigh Weldcore. Monolithic solids are best for thick-skinned dangerous game.

Johan Kotzé: There is such a wide variety of good bullets today it is very difficult to pick one, but I recommend any bullet that has been proven to keep its mass. Be sure to select a heavy-for-caliber bullet.

Corne Kruger: A good bonded bullet will never let you down.

Joof Lamprecht: I still like the Nosler Partitions for plains game, but there are so many products on the market now that it is difficult to choose. The Barnes brands do great on plains game and dangerous game. Only the best solids available should be used on thick-skinned big game.

Willem Mans: I am not too fond of Nosler Partitions after some of them have "partitioned" so well on game that not enough material stayed together to cause enough terminal destruction. All others are good, in my opinion.

Diethelm Metzger: My favorite bullet is the Trophy Bonded Bear Claw. And please note I do not get paid for saying this. Experience in the field has taught me this. Again, one has to have faith in what one is shooting. Most of the Partition bullets are good; also the new-generation Ballistic Tips are good. Many people bring Swift, Hornady, and Barnes bullets and their derivatives.

Peter Thormählen: In my opinion, the best bullet ever manufactured by a human being is the Trophy Bonded Bear Claw. Use their softpoints for plains game and the big cats, and Trophy Bonded Sledge Hammer solids for the thick-skinned animals—elephant, rhino, and hippo.

Woodleigh bullets are very close to Trophy Bonded. By the way, Trophy Bonded does not sponsor us; they are just my choice from experience.

Jamy Traut: For plains game, absolutely use premium-grade bullets. For slower calibers, like the .308 Winchester, the Nosler Partition is a great choice, while a strongly constructed bullet like the Swift A-Frame or Barnes X-Bullet is superior in the faster magnums.

For buffalo, the first shot should be taken with a premium-grade softpoint, and follow-up shots only with good solids. Again, the Barnes X-Bullet excels in this regard. For elephant, use strongly constructed solids only.

Rifles and Gear for a Namibian Safari

You might have only one shot at animals like this mountain zebra. Knowing your rifle and its ballistics is extremely important. (Photo courtesy of Willem Mans)

Gerrit Utz: Over the last few years I have had very good success with the Barnes X-Bullet. I personally believe in the strong softpoints on African game. I use them, combined with the same weight solids, in the bigger calibers for big game. On elephant and rhino we use only solids, but quite a few buffaloes we have hunted have been taken with the Barnes X-Bullet. Besides Barnes X-Bullet, the Swift A-Frame, Nosler, Brenneke TUG, and others do a very good job.

What I don't like to see are Silvertip and RWS or other similar softpoints.

We have had problems using full-metal-jacket bullets on elephants because their too-soft coating dismantles before they enter. That happens most on the frontal brain shots, and it causes us a lot of headaches.

John Wambach: Barnes X-Bullets have done very well, and so have Nosler Partitions. For big game, I recommend Barnes monolithic solids and Woodleigh solids.

Are there any rifles/calibers/optics you don't like to see?

Janneman Brand: A new rifle that the hunter has never used before!

Dirk de Bod: Yes, there are many rifle calibers we don't like to see. The hunter should let us know in advance what he will be bringing so we can approve it. Most of all, no muzzle brakes!

Kai-Uwe Denker: I cannot say that I dislike any particular rifles or optics. What I really dislike, however, is if clients carry around a loaded rifle and try to convince me that nothing can happen because of the infallible safety system of that particular rifle. Accidents nearly always happen due to human failure and not because of failing safety systems.

Peter Kibble: I am not fond of .30-06, .308, .270, and similar calibers, simply because they just do not have enough clout for most of our game. Only when you get a client who is an extremely good shot will these calibers suffice.

Johan Kotzé: It is the hunter's own choice as to what he brings; anything he feels comfortable with and trusts is likely do the job. Just one suggestion: Please think about your PH, who is going to be next to you when you pull the trigger, and stay away from muzzle brakes.

Corne Kruger: I personally hate Blaser rifles. About 50 percent of my clients who bring Blasers have problems with them, either from loose screws, actions that get stuck, or safeties that are too hard to get off. In terms of bullets, I am not a fan of Ballistic Tips.

Joof Lamprecht: I have had several bad experiences with clients' Blaser rifles discharging unexpectedly. The .308 Winchester caliber is for warfare and not for hunting game. Cheap scopes are out like cake in an orphanage. What I call "splat bullets," such as the Nosler Ballistic Tip, are unsuitable for African game. You are going to spend tens of thousands of dollars on your safari, so why skimp on your equipment and spoil your chances and your safari?

Willem Mans: Any rifle that is "not enough gun" for the animal to be hunted will never be acceptable.

Diethelm Metzger: Not really.

Peter Thormählen: The 7mm Remington Magnum. Most trophies we have lost happened with clients who used a 7mm magnum rifle.

Many professional hunters don't like to see muzzle brakes on their clients' rifles, as these devices increase the noise of the shot being fired to the point that it can damage the hearing of those standing nearby. (Photo courtesy of Johan Kotzé)

Jamy Traut: I am not a fan of most of the Weatherby calibers—too fast and too much recoil. I dislike muzzle brakes, but I also agree that the comfort of the client is a priority over that of the PH. Cheap scopes never give good, lasting results.

Gerrit Utz: I do not like the idea of a client bringing a brand-new rifle that he has never shot before, or that was only sighted in by the gunsmith. A hunter should be familiar with his rifle and know how it handles.

Also, cheap scopes on a rifle often cause problems, as the mount or the cross hair in the scope comes loose.

John Wambach: I don't like Weatherby calibers, as the high velocities generally aren't necessary, and many clients don't shoot them well. Also, don't bring inexpensive optics. Clients should have the best optics they can afford.

The common eland is the largest of Namibia's common plains game; bulls can weigh in excess of 1,200 pounds. Large calibers—.300 and up—are recommended. (Photo courtesy of Diethelm Metzger)

 ## What type of boots should a client wear?

Janneman Brand: Comfortable ones! I suggest ankle-high boots to keep out thorns and brush. Tall boots tend to get too hot!

Kai-Uwe Denker: Light, soft boots that are well worn.

Dirk de Bod: Good, well-worn-in hiking boots with gaiters or long pants.

Peter Kibble: It is of paramount importance to have comfortable footwear with soft soles and heels for quietness and comfort. There are many brands out there.

Johan Kotzé: Any type of boots that you can comfortably walk in for at least a couple of hours a day.

Corne Kruger: Any boots, as long as they are comfortable.

Joof Lamprecht: I personally recommend Russell boots. Ask them to show you the "Joof Lamprecht boot."

Willem Mans: Well-broken-in hiking boots.

Diethelm Metzger: Light boots that cover and support the ankle. The hunter should make sure that he can walk quietly. The shoes must be comfortable without causing sore feet after a long day of walking in the bush.

Peter Thormählen: I like Russell boots, as they are custom made. I spend lots of hours walking, and the Russells work well for me.

Jamy Traut: Lightweight shoes that have been broken in. If there is water to be crossed, two pairs of quick-drying shoes are a must. The second pair can be worn while the first pair dries out.

Gerrit Utz: I recommend boots of ankle height, that are lightweight, and are made of leather with a thick sole. It's important that the boot can breathe; otherwise, you cook your feet on long stalks.

Do not go out shopping for a pair of boots just before your safari, but bring the most worn-in and well-used boots that you have.

John Wambach: Noninsulated, 7-inch, full-leather boots with crepe soles of natural rubber for quiet stalking in the savanna, and heavy-duty, noninsulated boots for mountain backpack hunts.

 What clothing should a client wear—what colors, fabrics are best? Are shorts OK? How about camo?

Janneman Brand: Camo is allowed in Namibia. Ask your outfitter what the hunting area looks like and choose colors accordingly (olive khaki is almost always a good choice). Choose lightweight fabrics. Even in winter it warms up during the day; therefore, it's a good idea to layer your clothing. I prefer hunting with long trousers because you'll sometimes be crawling through the brush.

Kai-Uwe Denker: Light, durable clothing of khaki or green. Shorts should be worn only if the hunter is tough and has experience hiking in Africa. I don't like camo at all.

Dirk de Bod: Any good safari clothing in darker khaki or olive drab. Bright colors, such as white, yellow, and lighter versions of khaki, can adversely affect your hunt.

Peter Kibble: Shorts are fine. Dark green and brown clothing is preferable. Other dark colors are also fine.

On the other end of the spectrum and for small antelope like the klipspringer, a .243 or similar caliber is all that is required. (Photo courtesy of Diethelm Metzger)

Johan Kotzé: Camo would be my first choice, or anything similar to camo that blends well into the surroundings. Cool, light clothing that is breathable and comfortable while walking is also important. For early mornings and evenings, a warm jacket or fleece will do the job. During the winter months, long trousers are best because they protect you from thorns and grass seeds, but shorts will also work.

Corne Kruger: I am a BIG fan of camouflage, and it is allowed in Namibia. Dark colors also work. No light khaki, please!

Joof Lamprecht: Your background in Africa is dark during the entire year, so nothing beats dark green clothes made of heavy, strong cotton. Long sleeves and pants will protect you from stickers, hook thorns, insects, sunburn, and cold mornings and evenings. If you want to bleed, wear shorts. Your hat, which is the highest object on you, must be the same color. Camo is fine in Namibia, but not in some other African countries.

Willem Mans: Dull colors. Khaki seems good, as are dull camo patterns. Shorts are fine when the weather permits.

Diethelm Metzger: Dark clothing is important. Wear olive green or camo; dark khaki is also OK. Beware of light khaki as it sticks out like a sore thumb in the bush. Make sure that the clothing is quiet. During the winter months I would not recommend short pants. During the summer months one could wear shorts. I, however, always wear long jeans. Fleece is a very nice material but on a hunt I do not recommend it as everything sticks to it and thus makes it impractical. One should wear clothing that can be peeled off. Mornings are cold while the days may be warm. And the evenings may be freezing cold again. We can have temperatures as low as 10 degrees F during the nights and it will warm up to 65 degrees F or more during the day.

Peter Thormählen: Cotton clothes in dark colors (brown or green), no khaki. Shorts are fine. Zip-off pants work extremely well, as it is easy to put the pant legs back on when there are lots of thorns to walk through or when it gets cold. Camouflage works great.

Jamy Traut: Olive green works best all year-round; choose clothes made of a strong material. Camo is fine as well. Shorts are great if you don't mind getting a few scratches.

Gerrit Utz: The ideal outfit would be blue jeans or trousers made of a thick, strong material (thorns like getting caught on calves); a khaki, green, or brown long-sleeve shirt (to avoid sunburn on arms) made of a light fabric like cotton; a wide-brimmed hat that fits properly on the head so that wind does not blow it off; and socks and boots.

Avoid clothing in light beige, as this is like a signal to our game. All other hunting-clothing colors are fine. Camo is not necessary, but it is allowed in the country.

Shorts are fine, if you can take the thorns while stalking.

John Wambach: Camo is definitely best. Desert colors are best suited for our conditions and shorts can be worn. Sitka Gear in the Optifade Camo pattern is very good for both mountain and brush hunting.

Green and dark khaki-colored clothing is best for Namibian hunting. Also pack comfortable, soft-soled boots, a brimmed hat, a good binocular, and a rifle in the .300-caliber range.

 ## What are some other important items of gear a client should bring?

Janneman Brand: A wide-brimmed hat, sunblock, binocular (with a good strap), comfortable hunting boots, and knee pads.

Kai-Uwe Denker: A hat, sunscreen, and Band-Aids for blisters.

Dirk de Bod: A sweater and light jacket for evenings and early mornings, a cap or brimmed hat, gaiters to protect your socks from stickers, binocular with Bino Buddy or shoulder strap and lens cloth, gun cleaning kit, and a small flashlight. We provide a detailed packing list.

Rifles and Gear for a Namibian Safari

Peter Kibble: A good, durable, warm jacket. Shirts with collars to protect against the sun, a good hat, sunblock, good worn-in boots, and sunglasses.

Johan Kotzé: A flashlight always comes in handy; gloves and a beanie are good for the cold mornings or when driving in a vehicle. I also suggest a soft case for your rifle, a good binocular, a camera with enough memory, and, of course, if you need any special medications, bring them along. Most hunting areas are quite a long drive away from any pharmacy.

Corne Kruger: A good digital camera with plenty of memory, sunglasses, and a good binocular.

Joof Lamprecht: Three changes of hunting clothing will do as all camps have laundry service. Your travel outfit can double as street clothing if needed. A good 8X40 binocular with a heavy neck strap or harness is a must. A good, compact camera or, if you are big into photography, a professional kit. A good lock-blade knife or Leatherman is important. All the rest—shooting sticks, rangefinders, compasses, GPS, and other gadgets—your PH will have if he's worth his salt.

Willem Mans: A rifle and a good scope with which the client is well acquainted. People go on the safari of a lifetime with a rifle they have never hunted with before—even worse, they often have a brand-new scope as well, one which has not stood the test of time. This spells disaster!

Otherwise, I suggest bringing a good binocular, a hunting knife, camera, small flashlight, an alarm clock, sunscreen, and maybe a tripod-style shooting stick (always handy).

Diethelm Metzger: Good binoculars, camera (video and/or still), hat, warm jacket, sun protection, and lip balm.

Peter Thormählen: A good binocular, a good flashlight, sunscreen, a good hat, and waterproof matches or a lighter. A GPS doesn't hurt.

Jamy Traut: A good binocular that is small enough to be carried while walking, a small camera, a basic gun-cleaning kit, a lightweight backpack, a brimmed hat, sunblock, and sunglasses.

Gerrit Utz: I recommend a good 10X40 or 8X42 binocular, a good camera, 40–60 rounds of ammunition, a backpack to take in the hunting vehicle during the day for personal items you might need, good quality sunscreen for your face, arms, neck, and legs, sunglasses if your eyes are sensitive, a wide-brimmed hat, and lip balm. Also, I suggest bringing anti-itch cream for mosquito bites if you are hunting between February and May or from October to November.

Ask the Namibian Guides

John Wambach: A pack to carry water, such as a Camelbak, a wide-brimmed hat, sunglasses, sunscreen, binocular, daypack, and medical trip insurance.

 ## Is there anything a client shouldn't bring?

Janneman Brand: Do not bring excessive changes of clothing. Most outfitters have daily laundry services. Don't bring handguns as they are currently not allowed in Namibia. Most important, don't bring a bad attitude.

Dirk de Bod: Too many clothes. We do laundry every day.

Kai-Uwe Denker: Too much gear. If the stuff does not fit into a medium-size suitcase, it is definitely too much.

Many shots at game are taken from shooting sticks. Most PHs have these, or hunters can bring their own. (Photo courtesy of J. Scott Rupp)

Peter Kibble: Do not bring too much clothing; there is daily laundry service. No handguns, no automatic or semiautomatic weapons, and no crossbows, as these are illegal for hunting in Namibia.

Johan Kotzé: Bring what is necessary; we have a daily laundry service, so too many clothes aren't necessary. Keep the weight of your baggage under the weight limits of the airline, as there is no reason to spend extra money on overweight baggage.

Corne Kruger: A know-it-all attitude!

Joof Lamprecht: Do not bring a nasty or squeamish companion who does not want to be there.

Willem Mans: Bad manners and arrogance; a new, strange rifle with a loose scope; and bright clothing for the hunt. Rangefinders can be annoying, especially when a hunter misses a rare opportunity because he wasted time by using the rangefinder instead of believing the distance judgment of the PH right away!

Diethelm Metzger: Not too many changes of clothing as we have a daily laundry service. Do not bring fleece jackets for hunting, only for evening wear.

Peter Thormählen: Bad manners, rudeness, arrogance! We don't need that stuff on safari and in Africa. We like good manners and respect for our differences in culture. Isn't that why a client flies halfway around the world—to experience our country, culture, and differences in our way of doing things? Or is it to change us to be like his own country and culture?

Jamy Traut: Don't bring too many clothes. Most camps have daily laundry service.

Gerrit Utz: Too much clothing. We do laundry daily if needed, and bringing minimal changes of clothes makes the client's luggage weigh less.

John Wambach: A bad attitude; the client is here to have fun. Don't bring too many clothes or a cell phone.

Preparing for a Namibian Safari

Chapter 6

 How do you recommend hunters prepare for a safari? Any tips for shooting practice, etc?

Janneman Brand: Make sure you are fit for walking, and wear well-broken-in boots. Most hunts are done on foot. Make sure you are comfortable with your rifle and are familiar with its performance.

Dirk de Bod: Shoot your gun often from shooting sticks and from field positions to get good with it and learn the ballistics.

Kai-Uwe Denker: Three months before the onset of the safari, a client should begin practicing by walking at least ten miles twice a week and do short runs of 100 yards and a few push-ups. He should practice offhand shots at 100 yards once a week.

Peter Kibble: You should be completely familiar with your rifle and practice shooting with shooting sticks if you can, as this is the way most shots are taken on safari. However, if you are not familiar with the technique for shooting off shooting sticks, we can show you how to do it when you arrive.

Johan Kotzé: Familiarize yourself with the various species of African animals through books and videos. Do a lot of shooting and get to know your rifle. It's better to spend a little extra money on bullets for practicing at home, than on wounded game in Africa. (Most safari outfitters have a policy that you pay for any game that is wounded.)

Corne Kruger: Hunting is like any other sport: The more you practice, the luckier you get! Most hunters do not take this seriously, and then they pay the price when they are on safari. So the most important advice is to PRACTICE.

I always recommend that hunters do most of their shooting practice with small calibers because firing thirty shots from a bench with a .375 or another big gun will do nothing but teach you bad habits. Take a .22- or .17-caliber rifle and practice in different situations and from different shooting positions. Shooting from sticks is very important. I suggest buying three long sticks from a hardware store and tying them together about three inches from the top. These make great shooting sticks for practicing.

Extensive shooting practice is important before any safari, but that goes doubly if you're hunting dangerous game like buffalo. (Photo courtesy of Dirk de Bod)

Joof Lamprecht: Shoot three-shot groups at a paper target from 100 yards on a regular basis. Date each target and see if you notice any improvement. You can do some limited shooting off shooting sticks, but don't do too much as you won't like your grouping much. It makes no sense to go to the range once and shoot hundreds of rounds at cans and bottles.

Willem Mans: Get as fit as possible for long hikes. Make sure your rifle will shoot a 2-inch group and is sighted-in for 2 inches high at 100 yards.

Diethelm Metzger: One should be mentally prepared for going to a different country, a different continent, filled with different people, different cultures, and different food. Make sure that your mind-set is right to cope with this situation. Be prepared to have fun.

Also, go to the shooting range as often a possible to prepare well. Develop some physical fitness by walking every day. And make sure to get all paperwork in order well before the safari; i.e., passport or visas if necessary.

Peter Thormählen: Make sure your boots are well worn and broken in. Shoot your gun a lot, over a period of time. If possible, practice from shooting sticks, which you are going to use to hunt from in Africa. Then pack using our approved packing list.

Jamy Traut: Read as much as you can about the country, the species you are hunting, and the outfitter. Talk to hunters who have been on similar safaris in other places and at your destination. Look at worst-case scenarios, and mentally prepare yourself for those as well. Shoot often, from different positions, and not only from comfortable ones. Practice offhand at 20 to 50 yards and use shooting sticks as well, as all PHs use them. Make sure your rifle feeds well, consistently.

Gerrit Utz: At least a month before your safari, start making a daily habit of walking a mile, just to improve your physical condition. Take your wife with you and make it an outing. It makes a big difference once you are on safari.

Go to the shooting range as much as possible and practice with your chosen rifle. Also, practice shooting with a set of shooting sticks. Get to the point where you are comfortable with them and you know the right height to set the sticks so you can fire a good shot.

John Wambach: Practice your shooting from as many positions as possible, not just from the bench. Shoot from shooting sticks, prone, sitting, and on one knee. Another drill I recommend is to run a hundred yards, and then shoot in each of these positions.

 ## How far will most shots typically be?

Janneman Brand: Between 80 and 100 yards.
Dirk de Bod: Fifty to 250 yards.
Kai-Uwe Denker: Usually 150 to 250 yards.
Peter Kibble: Generally on safari, shots are anywhere from 60 yards to 200 yards depending on the situation and the type of animal that is being hunted.
Johan Kotzé: Anywhere from 50 to 250 yards.
Corne Kruger: About 150 to 250 yards for plains game, and up to 60 yards for big game.
Joof Lamprecht: It depends on the terrain. In wooded areas the shots will be between 50 and 100 yards. On the plains, I do not expect my clients to shoot over 200 yards.
Willem Mans: Generally, 150 to 220 yards.

Preparing for a Namibian Safari

Game usually doesn't wait around for a hunter to prepare, so be sure you're ready to shoot when your PH tells you to. (Photo courtesy of Diethelm Metzger)

Diethelm Metzger: We try to have our hunters shoot at animals between 90 and 165 yards. This is under normal circumstances. Our PHs are instructed to do the same. However, if the need arises and we have the confidence that the hunter can do it, it may happen that he will have to shoot at longer distances.

Peter Thormählen: For plains game, shots can be from 50 to 350 yards. Shots at dangerous game are taken at 10 to 50 yards.

Jamy Traut: That depends on the area and the species. Most plains game will be hunted between 80 and 150 yards. In the mountains and on the open plains, shots over 200 yards are not uncommon, but most PHs will get you in as close as possible, as that is what the hunt is all about.

For eland you may have to take an offhand shot at 30 yards, with no time to use shooting sticks. Practice is invaluable.

Elephants are typically taken between 10 and 30 yards. Leopards are usually shot from 40 to 80 yards, occasionally farther.

Gerrit Utz: Most shots on the ranch are between 100 to 150 yards, and in the concession they average 150 to 200 yards. Elephants are normally shot between 20 and 50 yards, and cats out of the blind, about 70 yards.

John Wambach: Shots vary from 40 yards to 300 yards, so know where your gun shoots at those distances.

 ## What are some of the most common mistakes you see hunters make on safari?

Janneman Brand: I commonly see shot placement that is too far back and too high. Also, some hunters get over-excited when taking their shots.

Dirk de Bod: Not knowing the gun or its ballistics and not being able to shoot it well. Second-guessing the PH and not listening to him are also common mistakes.

Kai-Uwe Denker: I can't really name any common mistakes.

Peter Kibble: Mistakes hunters make include not listening to the professional hunter and second-guessing his decisions, waving their hands around while stalking, flinching from and pulling shots, and looking up too soon after a shot instead of being prepared to shoot again.

Johan Kotzé: Clients overcompensate for long shots, holding too far over the animal. Also, when stalking animals, hunters should leave the binocular alone and be ready to shoot on the PH's OK.

Corne Kruger: Hunting for inches and not for the experience. I have seen so many people get so hung up on record books that they miss the whole experience and purpose of an African safari. Time and again, I have seen that it is the people who do not care about the size of their trophies who end up getting the big ones. Do not put your PH under pressure by demanding a certain trophy size.

Joof Lamprecht: One of the biggest mistakes is to turn down great trophies in the beginning of the safari in the hope of doing better later. One can always hope for a new world record, but very few of them are taken annually. So the possibility is there, but don't fool yourself and spoil your safari.

Another bit of advice: Do not think that you will shoot a 48-inch buffalo or a 65-inch kudu on your first safari. Any PH's nightmare is a client with the record book in one hand and a tape measure in the other. If you like the trophy and your PH says he thinks you should take it, take it! If your PH says he thinks you can do better, don't insist on shooting, listen to the man . . . you will in the future have the opportunity to improve on that first trophy, maybe even on the same safari. And for goodness sake, if the guy recommends that you use a

Practice your shooting with targets that look like game animals, such as those from the Perfect Shot series by Safari Press.

solid on the dangerous, thick-skinned animals, don't start messing around with some high-tech, brand-new bullets. He's been there and done that. Take his word for it. Trust your PH.

Willem Mans: The most common mistakes I see are: chambering a cartridge before it is needed, talking loudly, walking so noisily through the bush you sound like a bulldozer, and walking next to the PH or tracker instead of right behind him—that way, if you encounter a snake, it may get you and not your PH first! Another mistake is sometimes clients drink too much at night, and that affects the next day's hunt.

Diethelm Metzger: It's a mistake for clients to bring too much gear and too many guns, and it's a mistake to exaggerate their hunting and shooting ability.

Peter Thormählen: Telling the PH what to do. Also, panicking when things go wrong. This is absolutely normal, as clients do not have the same experience as the professional hunters.

Most shots at game animals in Namibia are not long, but animals such as the springbok can require a hunter to reach out to 300 yards or more. Scott Rupp's custom .25-06 was a perfect tool for the job.

Jamy Traut: Coming underprepared. Most people are excellent shots on the benchrest, but they have not practiced their field shooting enough.

A lot of hunters also make the mistake of shooting too far behind the shoulder of the animal. Most likely this is due to the slight difference in the anatomy of game in their home country and that of Africa.

Gerrit Utz: The following is the most common and annoying mistake that happens to me:

Scenario: We are stalking an antelope. The PH points out an animal and whispers to the hunter: "There is the big bull, take the shot."

The hunter, instead of shouldering his rifle, takes up his binoculars and looks at the bull just to "check . . ." And the chance is gone. Normally, an animal will give you a few seconds to fire your shot—waste any of those seconds, and the opportunity is often lost.

John Wambach: The most common mistake is when a client is not prepared to take a shot at any given time from any position, and then he misses an opportunity. Another mistake is second-guessing the PH. Remember, you are paying your PH to make the right calls.

 ## What advice would you give to someone who is on his/her first safari?

Janneman Brand: Pick the right outfitter for you and your family. Come with an open mind. Africa has so much to offer. Be more concerned about the hunt itself than the size of the trophies you collect. Your outfitter will do his best to get you the best available trophies. Enjoy yourself!

Dirk de Bod: Be well prepared and informed on all aspects of your safari. Study brochures and additional information provided by your outfitter.

Kai-Uwe Denker: To be honest, I very rarely had someone who was on his first safari. Clients who end up with me normally have quite some experience.

Peter Kibble: My advice for your first safari is to decide you want to really enjoy your experience and then to listen to the PH's instructions. If you take this advice, you should have a great time and a very memorable experience.

Johan Kotzé: Put your trust in your PH and enjoy the safari experience.

Corne Kruger: Go out and have fun. Forget about how big the animals must be, and just go out there and have a great hunt. You will go home with the best trophy of all—great memories.

Joof Lamprecht: Be prepared to have the time of your life. Relax, forget about the office, and have fun.

Willem Mans: Try your best to be a nice and friendly personality. Always behave well. Follow the guidance of your PH—he is there to make your hunt as successful and unforgettable as possible. Be a good shot, and be patient.

Diethelm Metzger: Book with someone who has been proven to be trustworthy (check that reference list) or someone you feel you can trust (once you have met him at a show). Go out there to have fun and let yourself be guided. That is what you are paying for. Do not worry; we will get you to the desired trophy, or an even better one!

Ask the Namibian Guides

Peter Thormählen: Spend a lot of time researching to find the short list of good, reputable outfitters, and then talk to their references. If you can, meet the outfitter in person at a hunting convention, and make sure the outfitter knows what your specific needs are for your safari. For example, are you hunting for big trophies only, are you hunting in general, are you hunting and touring, or are you taking a safari as a honeymoon? Make sure the outfitter assigns the professional hunter that is most compatible with your (and your family's) personalities and goals. After all, it is your party since you are paying for it!

Jamy Traut: Make sure you are comfortable with your rifle and caliber combination. Make sure you are fit enough for the type of safari you booked. Practice often, and read enough about your potential safari. And remember that how much you enjoy the safari will depend on you.

Gerrit Utz: Namibian game is tough and fast. Do not go and book your safari and then, a day before you leave, pull out your rifle and blow the dust off it and pack it in your rifle case. Prepare, and the rewards are much better.

John Wambach: Have fun, and take everything that happens in stride. Remember, you are in the bush. Your safari is not a rehearsed play, nor is it a supermarket.

 ## What's the best time of year to come?

Janneman Brand: April through September.
Dirk de Bod: Mid-March to mid-November.
Kai-Uwe Denker: The dry season.
Peter Kibble: The season stretches from 1 February to 31 November, and all the months in the season are good. My preferences are March, April, May, June, August, September, October, and November. During those last months, the days are long, so you hunt in early morning and late afternoon. The nights are cool and the days hot. In July, the days are short and it is very cold in the mornings; it warms up a bit, and then is very cold at night.
Johan Kotzé: April through September.
Corne Kruger: Any time from February to November is good; it just depends on what sort of temperatures you like.
Joof Lamprecht: From 1 February to 30 November. The months of December and January are the closed season.
Willem Mans: The cool/colder months from April to September.

Diethelm Metzger: April through September.

Peter Thormählen: March through September are the most beautiful months. But for the big cats, the period of June through November is best. Plains game can be hunted any time from March through November.

Jamy Traut: Again, that depends on species and area. The visiting hunter will see more game during the drier months of May through September. If kudu is a priority, give some thought to hunting during the rut (mid-May to mid-June). However, in Namibia we are fortunate to have a lot of game all over, and you will see enough to keep you happy, no matter when you come.

Gerrit Utz: It depends on the type of hunt you are going for—plains game or dangerous game—and what area you are going to.

The official trophy-hunting season starts 1 February and runs through 30 November. Generally, one can say that hunting is good from mid-April to mid-October. Before April it is still the rainy season, and you might get some rainy days. After October, it is very hot and the hunting time in a day is shortened due to the great midday heat, which lasts three to four hours.

Moon phase is also a concern. Depending on the species to be hunted, less moon or bright moon is better.

John Wambach: April to November.

Arriving and Departing

Chapter 7

 What happens when a client arrives in Namibia? Where does he arrive and how does he get to camp?

Janneman Brand: Clients arrive at the international airport in Windhoek. I will be there to meet and drive the client to Kalahari Safari. On arriving in Namibia, I will take care of all the logistics and hunting requirements, so the client only has to sit back and relax.

Dirk de Bod: When clients arrive at Windhoek International, I personally pick them up and take them directly to the camp, which is one hour north of the airport.

Kai-Uwe Denker: The client will normally arrive at Hosea Kutako International Airport and will have to go through Customs and clear his rifle. The process is very uncomplicated.

Flights from Johannesburg, South Africa, and Frankfurt, Germany, land daily at Hosea Kutako International Airport outside of the capital city of Windhoek.

Windhoek, population 250,000, is the largest city in Namibia; it is clean and modern.

If he visits our big-game areas in the northeast, he will proceed by charter, and we will pick him up at the airstrip near camp. For our hunting areas in western Namibia, we pick up our clients at the international airport and travel by car into the hunting areas.

Peter Kibble: Most clients arrive at Hosea Kutako International Airport. We are always there to greet them and transport them to camp. Obviously we return them to the airport at the end of the hunt. Being on the spot allows us to assist if there is a problem.

Johan Kotzé: Namibia's international airport is called Hosea Kutako. All flights coming into Namibia land there. You will be picked up by your PH, or by a representative of the outfitter, at the airport. From there, someone will drive you to your hunting camp.

Corne Kruger: Clients arrive at Hosea Kutako Airport near Windhoek. We pick you up at the airport and then drive you 45 minutes to our main camp for your first day.

Ask the Namibian Guides

Joof Lamprecht: Clients fly into our international airport, Hosea Kutako, which is twenty minutes from our capital, Windhoek. Customs clearance and gun import is very easy, and a document with limited information needs to be filled in. It is customary for Namibian outfitters to pick their clients up personally.

Willem Mans: Our clients are picked up at Upington Airport in the Republic of South Africa and then transferred to the ranch by road. We will cross the border, and upon entering Namibia we will secure a Namibian gun permit for you.

Diethelm Metzger: The hunter arrives at Hosea Kutako International Airport, which is situated close to Windhoek. Most flights are from Frankfurt, Germany, or Johannesburg, South Africa. After landing, the hunter has to walk to the arrival hall where he has to fill in an arrival form; he then proceeds through Immigration. The personnel there should be greeted in a friendly way, but no small talk. They do not appreciate that. They will ask for the physical address of the hunter's stay, which the outfitter should have provided.

Once done with Immigration, the hunter proceeds to the baggage claim area and retrieves his suitcase or luggage. At that point he needs to find a small office with a sign that reads "Arms and Ammunition." (If he looks back toward Immigration, he will see this office.) That is where one identifies the gun case and waits to fill in a temporary gun license/permit. Once this has been achieved, the hunter proceeds through Customs and Excise, preferably the green door. The PH, wearing a Makadi Safaris shirt, will be waiting right outside to meet him. He will then drive him to the hunting lodge, about one hour from the airport.

Peter Thormählen: Clients arrive at Hosea Kutako International Airport in the capital city of Windhoek. To get to our Kaokoland concession for desert leopard, desert lion, and plains game, most clients travel by road, but some take a private charter plane to the concession.

Jamy Traut: All flights start and end in Windhoek, the capital. The PH or a representative of Jamy Traut Hunting Safaris will meet the client and drive him to camp. If the arrival is late, the client will spend the night in Windhoek. If air charter is part of the travel, the pilot will meet the client upon his arrival at the airport.

Gerrit Utz: Clients arrive at Windhoek International Airport. There, I or an employee of mine will meet the client at the arrival hall and drive him to the hunting area.

Roads and infrastructure in Namibia, both in the cities and in rural areas, are some of the best in Africa.

Alternatively, if the client is scheduled to fly to the concession by charter, the pilot awaits the client with a signboard with his name on it, collects him at the arrival hall, and flies him to the concession area. There I will meet him at the landing strip and take him to camp.

John Wambach: After arriving in Windhoek, you will need to clear your guns at Customs; it is a very simple process of filling out one form with your gun details and the address of where you will be staying for the duration of your hunt. Your outfitter will pick you up and either drive you to camp, or you will take a charter flight to camp.

 ## How much should a client tip a PH? (Discuss both plains game and dangerous-game hunts, if applicable.)

Janneman Brand: Tipping is totally up to the discretion of the client. No one is entitled to a tip—it should always be considered a bonus.

A typical road-hazard sign in Namibia.

Dirk de Bod: It is up to the client and should be based on how he feels at the end of the safari. On plains game, typically 5 to 10 percent of the invoice amount is common; on dangerous game, around 5 percent is an average tip, but again it is up to the client.

Kai-Uwe Denker: The hunter should use his own discretion regarding what he thinks was "earned," and it should also be based on how much he can afford.

Peter Kibble: No matter if it is a plains-game or dangerous-game hunt, the work and effort is the same. PHs usually get U.S. $100 per day; should one want to give more, it is entirely at the discretion of the client.

Johan Kotzé: Someone once said a tip is to reward and encourage good service. It all depends on the number of days you hunt and the number of trophies you take. I think a good guideline is to work on about 10 percent of the total cost of the hunt. But at the end of the day, it is a personal choice.

Corne Kruger: This is up to the client and his budget.

Joof Lamprecht: The PH's tip depends on his performance and your generosity. On dangerous-game hunts, the tip amount is normally double that of a plains-game safari.

Willem Mans: I suggest tipping 2.5 to 5 percent of the hunt cost.

Diethelm Metzger: A guideline, I would say, is about U.S. $800 to $1,000 per 10-day hunt. This applies to both plains-game and dangerous-game hunts. However, it could be less if the hunter is not satisfied. I would even suggest that if the hunter was not happy with the hunt at all, no tip should be forthcoming. But the outfitter should also then be informed about the situation.

Peter Thormählen: This depends highly on the type of safari; for example, whether it is a plains-game or dangerous-game safari. In Namibia, we probably have the best professional hunters money can buy, so my tip suggestion may differ from that of other outfitters. Generally, I would say for a seven- to ten-day plains-game safari, a tip of U.S. $700–$1,000 is usual. For a fourteen-day leopard or lion safari, tip between U.S. $2,000–$3,500.

Jamy Traut: I think this is personal to each client, but if I have to put a number to it, between U.S. $50 and $100 per day of hunting . . . IF the PH has worked hard for the client.

Gerrit Utz: For a seven-day-plains-game hunt, a tip of approximately U.S. $200 to $500 is usual. For a dangerous-game hunt (14 days or more), a tip of approximately U.S. $1,000 is usual.

I personally think that too much emphasis is placed on tips, and they are often overdone. All the staff is receiving a market-related salary, and the tip should only be a thank-you for outstanding extra effort. The tip should not outbalance the salary. It very often makes the staff unhappy about their "bad salaries." Many discussions have happened after hunts in outfits between the staff and the outfitter about tips not being high enough, but never about the extra effort not put into the hunt by the staff.

John Wambach: Tips are very personal. I have had clients tip me $1,000 for a plains-game hunt, and then I've had very successful elephant hunts where the client left a $500 tip. It is merely a token, and the way I see it, it is the gesture and not really the amount that counts.

 ## How much should a client tip the camp staff—the trackers, skinners, cooks?

Janneman Brand: Again, tipping is totally up to the discretion of the client. It depends on the client's experience with the staff.

Dirk de Bod: It is up to the client. The PH can advise him at the end of the safari and then he can give it to the staff personally.

Kai-Uwe Denker: The hunter should discuss this with his PH in camp.

Ask the Namibian Guides

Peter Kibble: In our operation, skinners, trackers, cooks, and camp staff all work extremely hard by putting a lot of effort into seeing that the client is comfortable, well fed, has his laundry done, etc. The trackers and skinners also work very hard, making sure all of your instructions are followed. They take great pride in what they do. The going rate is U.S. $20 per day for each of the staff.

Johan Kotzé: You can personally tip your driver and tracker because they are the people who will be with you every day. Five to 10 dollars a day would be appropriate. Always remember that there are a lot of people behind the scenes as well: skinners, laundry personnel, cooks, maids, etc. Skinners also get $5 to $10 per day; camp staff members $3 to $5 per day.

Corne Kruger: Again, this is up to the client and his budget.

Joof Lamprecht: Do not, on the last day of your safari, start handing out tips to staff as you are going to miss some staff and cause a problem for your PH. Ask him how many staff members there are and decide how much each one should get. Good PHs have a seniority list, and tips are distributed fairly.

Willem Mans: Tip the staff a total of 2½ to 5 percent of the cost of the hunt.

Diethelm Metzger: Per hunter, the tip should be around U.S. $300 to $400, split among the various members of the staff.

Peter Thormählen: I know I differ with most outfitters on tips for camp staff, tracker, and skinner as I believe that the most important people after the PH are your tracker and your skinner. If the tracker does not find your trophy, and if the skinner does not skin it properly, how successful was your safari? Will you be left with only photos or a damaged, poorly skinned trophy against your wall?

For a plains-game safari of seven to ten days, I suggest the following: Tip for the camp staff U.S. $400 for the entire camp staff; tip for the tracker U.S. $200 to $400; tip for the skinner, U.S. $200 to $400.

For a dangerous-game safari of fourteen to twenty-one days, I suggest: Tip for the camp staff U.S. $400 to $500 for the whole camp; tip for the tracker U.S. $300 to $400; tip for the skinner U.S. $300 to $400.

Jamy Traut: Tip U.S. $400 to $600 for every week of hunting for a staff group of between four and six people. If a specific tracker or other member of the staff excelled in the eyes of the client, the tip could double for the person in question.

Arriving and Departing

Trophies are usually skinned, caped, and butchered in the field or at the safari headquarters.
(Photo courtesy of James Reed)

Ask the Namibian Guides

Gerrit Utz: The trackers usually get about U.S. $50 a week; the skinners, camp cleaning staff, and so on get about U.S. $30 a week. The cook (depending on the quality of the food) about U.S. $50 a week.

Of course, extra appreciation may be warranted for staffers who made special efforts that led to success or additional comfort. Only tip at the end of the safari, and be sure to discuss it with the PH!

John Wambach: On a plains-game safari we recommend a tip of $50 per person. On a big-game safari, $100 per person and, for your trackers, $150.

 Should tips be in U.S. dollars or Namibian currency? Are gifts for staff appropriate?

Janneman Brand: The staff always appreciates gifts. Tips can be in U.S. dollars; the outfitter will exchange it into Namibian currency for his staff.

Dirk de Bod: U.S. dollars are OK as they can be exchanged for Namibian currency, saving the client the trouble. Gifts like clothing are OK, but most prefer cash.

Kai-Uwe Denker: Tips should be in South African rand or Namibian dollars and gifts are appropriate, especially if the hunter has been there before and feels he wants to give something special. In general, however, clients should come to hunt and not make their journey into a charity mission.

Peter Kibble: Tips should be in U.S. dollars, euros, or rands. As far as gifts are concerned, if a client wants to give any kind of gift, this is fine, but do not use gifts as tips.

Johan Kotzé: Most clients tip in dollars. Gifts are more than welcome for the staff. A lot of clients will leave their hunting gear for the staff—shirts, trousers, jackets, etc.—and that is really appreciated by our staff.

Corne Kruger: The type of currency does not matter. Yes, the staff members really love gifts.

Joof Lamprecht: Both currencies are fine. Lock-blade knives are always welcome in Africa.

Willem Mans: Dollars are fine, and gifts are acceptable as long as they do not replace tips completely.

Diethelm Metzger: To make it easier for the client, all fees, including tips, should be settled in U.S. dollars. Gifts are also fine and are very much appreciated.

The meat of all animals shot on safari is utilized in some way; nothing goes to waste. (Photo courtesy of James Reed)

Peter Thormählen: It is best to tip in U.S. dollars. Gifts are great as long as they do not replace the tips. It is embarrassing when clients give a skinner a knife as tip, for example. They know what the values are of knives, Leathermans, pants, shirts, jackets, and the like! A gift is a gift, if it is a gift. A tip is a tip, and a way to say "thank you" for a great service.

Jamy Traut: If tips are in dollars, let the PH exchange it for you. Staff members welcome gifts.

Gerrit Utz: It does not matter. If the client gives the tip in dollars, I will convert the money to rand/Namibian dollars and give it with the salary to my employees.

Gifts are always welcome among staff, but it is important that all of them get something. Not only the tracker or the guy who is around you in camp, but also the "invisible" staff members, such as the cleaning staff, the skinner, the kitchen guy, etc.

John Wambach: Tips can be in dollars or rands. Gifts are always a nice way of showing appreciation.

Describe the process you use for preparing clients' trophies for shipment. What do hunters need to know about this process?

Janneman Brand: You (the client) and I will fill out the taxidermy forms together. Upon your departure, we make sure all hides and horns are marked, measured, and prepared for collection by the taxidermist. The taxidermist then collects everything from the ranch and takes it to Windhoek. He will contact you before he starts the export process.

Kai-Uwe Denker: Skins are salted and dried, and skulls are cleaned. At the end of the season, all trophies (if necessary) are put into quarantine, and thereafter delivered to the shipping agent who will see to all the other requirements before the trophy can be shipped.

Dirk de Bod: We do the skinning, salting, disinfecting, cleaning, and drying, and then take it to a taxidermist for shipping.

Peter Kibble: We undertake all the field preparations of trophies, including skinning, and deliver them for mounting or shipping to our taxidermist in Windhoek.

Johan Kotzé: We do only the skinning and salting of the trophies on the farm. The client will fill in a detailed form with his address, a listing of the trophies, whether they are to be mounted in Namibia, and if so, how they should be mounted by the taxidermist. The taxidermist who will do the shipping picks up the trophies from the outfitter, and then they get in contact with the client to arrange payment and confirm details.

Corne Kruger: Clients should know that we use only the best when it comes to trophy preparation. A highly professional team skins the animals. Skins and skulls are salted and dried. Then they are delivered to the taxidermist, who cleans them, dips them, and ships them.

Joof Lamprecht: Trophies are prepared using the so-called "field preparation," which means that all the skins are skinned to the prescribed style for taxidermy preparation, salted, dried, and folded in a parcel shape. The skulls are cleaned and rendered in a sterile condition to international veterinary health regulations. Once the trophies are delivered to the freight agent and cataloged, the PH's responsibility ends.

Willem Mans: We clean, dry, and dip trophies completely as part of the price so that they are ready for a taxidermist to proceed with the tanning/

Arriving and Departing

Bazaars like this one are good places to shop for wood carvings, baskets, and other traditional items at the end of the safari.

mounting. The trophies are then shipped to the exporter, who will export the trophies to the client.

Diethelm Metzger: Once an animal is shot, all parts of the trophy are tagged right there in the field. The hunter's wishes for the type of mount for the specific trophy are carefully recorded right away in order to prohibit any confusion at a later stage. While the hunter is continuing with his hunt, the driver will take the trophy and animal back to camp to be skinned and butchered.

Expert skinners will skin the animal to the hunter's wishes. All skin parts will be washed and salted. The skull and horns will be cleaned thoroughly and later buried in salt. After two days, the skins will be hung to dry, cleaned once more, and then folded and stored in the skinning shed. The skulls will also be cleaned and stored on a rack outside. Within seven days of the hunter's departure, the trophies will be taken to a taxidermist in Windhoek for further professional cleaning and dipping. This is required to be able to ship the trophies internationally.

Skulls and horns are preserved in a salt shed.

Before the hunter leaves Makadi Safaris, I carefully record all instructions regarding the trophies. The trophies will then be delivered to the taxidermist for dip and ship or full trophy preparation. The taxidermist will contact the hunter once trophies have been received. He again will reconfirm all instructions concerning the treatment of the trophies. At this point in time, a 50 percent deposit payment will be required by the taxidermist to be able to start work on the trophies. Once the taxidermist is finished with his work, he will contact the shipping agent who will again take care of all special permits to ship the trophies to the United States.

Peter Thormählen: The most important time for a trophy is when it is in the hands of the skinner, as the skinner has to make sure the skin has no meat or fat on it, that it is not cut, that it is properly salted and dried in the shade, and that it is folded so that it can arrive safely at the taxidermy shop. There it will either be prepared for raw shipment to the client, or the actual taxidermy will be done in Africa, depending on the client's choice.

The taxidermist will forward the trophies to a shipper, who will ship it either by air or by sea, depending on the client's wishes.

Jamy Traut: After field preparation (skinning and initial cleaning of the skull), the trophies are put in a brine solution overnight. The next day, the skins are put in a salt bed (both sides), and the skulls are cleaned. As much flesh as possible is removed from the skulls, and all cavities, including the brain, are cleaned. By keeping the skulls soaked in water for an extended period, all remaining flesh, fat, and blood is removed. Skins are folded after a few days to a size of approximately one square meter. Skulls from game taken in areas that are considered foot and mouth disease regions, like the Caprivi, are put in caustic soda for one hour.

The dipping and packing process involves the skull being put in peroxide for bleaching, and the skins are softened again to ensure that all fat and meat have been removed. Then they are put in a strong brine solution with debacteriocyte and fungicide. The skins are then dried again and folded for packing.

Gerrit Utz: What hunters need to know is that all of their trophies are immediately and clearly marked with their names on durable tags especially made for trophies and skins. This way, nothing is lost or mixed up.

The general process is that the animal gets skinned, and the skin is cleaned of any meat and washed in a salt bath. After that, it is thickly packed in salt and dried.

Skulls are cleaned of meat and put in a large barrel with water so that the remaining meat can rot off. After this, they are scraped clean and put in a heap of coarse salt. With this process, any fat is drawn out of the bone of the skull.

From there it goes to the Namibian taxidermist or the skulls get cleaned in peroxide (the dipping process), and then sent on to the forwarding agent.

John Wambach: After the capes are skinned properly, they are placed in a heavy brine solution with antiseptic to kill off bacteria. Afterward, they are salted and then dried, tagged for each client, and transported to the taxidermist.

What to Expect

Chapter 8

 Describe a typical hunting day on one of your safaris.

Janneman Brand: We wake you up just after 5 A.M. We have breakfast as the day breaks and then head out to the field. We will spot and stalk until we have shot the desired trophy. After taking photos, we head to the skinning shed. Should it still be early in the morning, we will head out to the field again; otherwise, we will return to the lodge for lunch and a nap. We return to the main camp every day for lunch, unless we are on a stalk. About 3 P.M., we head out again and hunt until sunset. Upon our return, the campfire will be burning and we will sit down for a sumptuous dinner by candlelight.

Many of Namibia's hunting areas feature luxury accommodations such as this comfortable lodge featuring a traditional thatched roof at Kalahari Safari. (Photo courtesy of Janneman Brand)

What to Expect

In wilderness regions, basic tent accommodations are the norm. This is a client tent in Bushmanland. (Photo courtesy of Kai-Uwe Denker)

Dirk de Bod: We wake up at sunrise, have breakfast, leave camp in the hunting vehicle, and start hunting. We will spot game from the car and then get out to stalk. We come back to camp for lunch, and then head back out around three o'clock and hunt until dark.

Kai-Uwe Denker: On big-game safaris we normally have breakfast well before sunrise and then leave camp to stay out for the entire day, and in most cases we return only after sunset. We carry along sandwiches, oranges, and water while we're out tracking. At times we leave camp on foot; at other times we drive to some faraway water hole where we hope to find fresh tracks and from there we commence on foot. There is no cool box in the car, and during the day, we only drink water. When hunting plains game, we normally return to camp to rest during the hottest part of the day.

Peter Kibble: Normally you rise around 6:00 A.M., have breakfast, and then hunt during the morning, returning to camp for a light lunch. Rest, and then go out in the afternoon, returning in the early evening for drinks around a warm fire followed by a candlelit dinner with superb wine. This is the main meal of the day. Some days, if we are hunting farther away from the main camp, we will take a picnic lunch or have a barbecue in the bush, returning to camp in the evening. We carry drinks and refreshments in the car.

Johan Kotzé: The day starts before sunrise, with breakfast. We then drive off and start hunting. Because the area is so big, we drive around in the vehicle looking for trophies. When we spot an animal, we get out of the vehicle to stalk. Sometimes we will hike into areas where the animals are known to be, like riverbeds, plains, etc. Usually we will go back to camp to have lunch, and then head off to hunt in the afternoon and hunt until sunset.

Corne Kruger: Hunters will get up just before sunrise and have a great breakfast on the deck while watching the sun rise. We start hunting twenty minutes after sunrise. Hunters will travel in a Land Cruiser during the hunt, and all hunting is done by spot and stalk. Lunch is served around noon, and the hunt resumes at 3:00 P.M. and continues until sunset.

Joof Lamprecht: A typical day starts before sunrise with a wake-up call and beverages of the client's choice delivered to his bedroom. Once everyone is dressed and ready, breakfast is served in the dining area. After breakfast, the hunt starts. Around midday, all return to the lodge for lunch and a siesta. Beverages are served again at midafternoon and the hunt continues. We return to the lodge after sunset, where sundowners are served around the fire pit. We discuss the day's events, and then we move to the dining area to have dinner. A traditional drumbeat announces dinner, which is always a candlelit, three-course gourmet feast.

Top-quality South African wines, international brands of whiskey, gin, vodka, and world-class Namibian beer, as well as a variety of soft drinks and pure fruit juices are available in camp. Most clients retire around nine o'clock.

Willem Mans: After having a good breakfast, we leave camp at least half an hour before sunrise by pickup truck (known here as a bakkie). We spot and stalk for trophies until noon, and then we have a picnic lunch and take a siesta till about 3:00. We'll continue with the hunt until after sundown and return to camp for a great dinner.

Diethelm Metzger: During our winter, the sun rises at 6:00 A.M. Breakfast will be before that, at 5:30, so the hunting party can leave at sunrise. The hunters will always have a driver and a PH with them. Once the hunting area has been reached, they will get out of the vehicle and start walking, tracking, and stalking. The amount of walking per day is geared toward the hunter's

What to Expect

Hunters never know what they might spot next from the safari vehicle. (Photo courtesy of Diethelm Metzger)

abilities. The PH will try to find animals, stalk them with the hunter, identify a trophy, and then, we hope, the hunter will shoot it.

Once the animal is down, the PH will wish the hunter *Weidmannsheil* (hail to the hunter), the animal will receive its last bite (a German hunting tradition), and photos will be taken. As mentioned before, the hunters will proceed with hunting while the driver takes the animal back to camp so that it can be skinned as soon as possible.

The hunting vehicle always carries a cool box with drinks, a lunch box, and a coffee box to ensure that the hunters will never go hungry. Lunch will usually be offered in a blind or under a shady tree at a water hole. That provides the hunters with the opportunity of observing game at the water hole while having their meal.

Usually the hunters will stay in the blind for two to three hours, depending how much action and fun is happening at the water. In the afternoon, it will be walk-and-stalk again, scanning of hillsides, etc., until the sun sets. Upon your arrival in camp, a warm fire will be going, the drinks will be waiting at the bar, and a gourmet meal will be served after a long day of hunting.

A gourmet chef prepares a wild game dinner at Hunters Namibia Safaris. (Photo courtesy of Joof Lamprecht)

Peter Thormählen: In the winter months, clients are awakened with a hot cup of coffee or tea in their tent or chalet around 5 A.M., and in the summer months we wake clients at 4 A.M. After toast, cereal, fruit, and yogurt, the hunting party takes off to start hunting. All our hunting cars are equipped with a folding table with four canvas chairs, a cooler box, a complete lunch box with cutlery for six clients, coffee presses, tablecloths, etc., as our clients normally enjoy lunch in the bush. We do not serve our clients lunch on a car's bonnet, or in the back of the car.

The hunting group normally returns to camp after sunset. Clients are welcomed back with snacks and a drink, and then they have time to shower or refresh before dinner. Red and white wine is served with dinner.

Jamy Traut: A typical day varies tremendously according to the species we are tracking and the area in which we will be hunting. In essence, we get an early start after a light breakfast. For game that requires tracking from water holes (eland and occasionally elephant), we try to be on the tracks before sunrise while the game is still feeding and thus easier to approach.

What to Expect

For most other plains game, it will be a matter of spot-and-stalk, covering ground either with a vehicle or on foot. In the central mountain area, a standard approach will be to choose an elevated area and do a lot of glassing to identify potential targets, after which the stalk takes place.

Gerrit Utz: Around sunrise, we have breakfast at the farmhouse, and after finishing, leave for the hunt. The 4x4 truck will be waiting for us. In the concession, we spend the midday hours out in the bush and do not return to camp. We take our lunch under a shady tree, and depending how hot the day is, we take a rest or a nap until it starts to get cooler. At sunset we return to camp for our dinner and enjoy to the time together at the fire. On the ranch, normally we come in for lunch and leave after a short rest to hunt again until dark.

John Wambach: We get up before sunrise, have a cup of coffee and some cereal, and then we head out into the field. We look for vantage points where we glass to find the species we are seeking. Then we do a stalk until we get the animal.

On a backpack hunt, we leave the trailhead with our packs and then hike to the area where I have scouted for the species we will be hunting. There, we put up a spike camp and then get going the next day before sunrise, hiking up into higher ground and glassing for the species we are after. After shooting an animal, we will skin it out and then pack everything back to the trailhead.

 Describe your camps/facilities.

Janneman Brand: Kalahari Safari offers luxury accommodations for the discerning hunter and his family. All rooms are en suite, with bath and separate shower. Private verandas overlook the water hole. We also have a swimming pool, as well as a bush spa offering spa treatments.

Dirk de Bod: We have a luxurious tented safari camp with en-suite bathrooms. Located on the bank of a dry riverbed, it overlooks the picturesque bushveld. Clients may enjoy a sundowner by the fire while watching wildlife at the nearby water hole.

Kai-Uwe Denker: We have tented camps. This means the clients sleep in tents that are mosquito- and snake-proof. Each tent has a veranda in front, and there is a bucket shower and a long-drop toilet near each tent. The camps have a basic *lapa* (thatched outdoor entertainment area) and kitchen. Most of the cooking is done on the campfire. We have cooling

Sitting around the campfire in the evening, swapping stories, is an integral part of the safari experience. (Photo courtesy of Joof Lamprecht)

facilities with propane gas. Our camps have no electricity in any form. There is no generator.

Peter Kibble: We have a luxury tented camp with bathrooms attached—all this set in an acacia woodland next to a mountain.

Johan Kotzé: We have a lodge with four spacious double rooms with en-suite bathrooms that include a toilet, shower, and Jacuzzi. The lodge also has a restaurant, bar, kitchen, living area, TV area, lounge, and an outside *lapa* with a swimming pool.

Corne Kruger: We have a luxury lodge at our main hunting area, with a magnificent view of rolling hills and wild animals visible from our porch, as well as satellite television and wi-fi in the common areas. Our area in the south features luxury farmhouse-style accommodation. At our concession in northwestern Namibia, we offer luxury tented camps for the entire family to enjoy. The cry of a hyena, the roar of a lion, and a crackling campfire sets the tone after an exciting day's hunt.

Joof Lamprecht: The two Hunters Namibia Safaris Lodges, Main Lodge and Lake Lodge, are run in the classic, elegant style of traditional safari camps. The lodges are spacious buildings of natural stone with thatched roofs, designed to blend in with the surrounding rocky kopjes and vast savannas.

What to Expect

Both lodges offer guest suites with en-suite bathrooms with basins, flush toilets, and large showers. The extra length beds are solid wood with thick, firm mattresses, down duvets, and pillows. Bedside tables, reading lamps, a luggage rack, rifle cabinet, large wardrobe, comfortable chairs, a desk, ceiling fan, balcony furniture complete the comfortable, distinctly safari-style rooms. Two of the loft suites at the Main Lodge feature stone fireplaces, and one of the suites offers a connecting room for children.

At the Main Lodge, sun decks with hammocks and deck chairs, the swimming pool, and summerhouse were specially designed to make the safari more enjoyable for nonhunters and children. Water holes are strategically placed near both lodges to allow game viewing and photography from your suite and sun decks.

Although we strongly recommend that you relax and unwind during your safari, fax, cellular phone reception, telephone, and Internet facilities, as well as satellite television are available for clients who may wish to make use of them.

Willem Mans: Clients stay in thatched en-suite chalets that are located fifty meters from the main house.

Diethelm Metzger: We have five double rooms, each with its own bathroom. They are very comfortable. Our camp also has a swimming pool, dining area with bar, a nice garden and entertainment area, and outside grilling facilities.

Peter Thormählen: At the moment we have a communal concession in Kaokoland of 495,000 acres with desert lion, desert leopard, spotted hyena, and cheetah on quota, as well as plains-game species—oryx (gemsbok), springbok, Hartmann zebra, southern greater kudu, klipspringer, Cape eland, and steenbok. This concession features a tented camp and contains three client tents with en-suite showers with hot and cold water and flush toilets; a mess tent with a bar, a living area, and dining table; a kitchen tent; the camp manager's tent, a PH tent; and a staff village where the community staff as well as the trackers and skinners have their tents. There is an outside fire pit where clients enjoy snacks, drinks, and lots of fun moments.

In the central Kalahari, we hunt on a private property of 12,500 acres where we have black and blue wildebeest, red hartebeest, blesbok, waterbuck, springbok, black-faced impala, southern impala, Cape eland, springbok, and Burchell zebra on quota. Accommodation in this concession is a hunting lodge with rooms for the clients and all the necessary facilities—bathrooms, sleeping rooms, and so on.

Ask the Namibian Guides

A Burchell zebra races a common eland. (Photo courtesy of Jofie Lamprecht)

Jamy Traut: The Caprivi camp is a typical old-style tented safari camp (nonpermanent). It has all the amenities, including en-suite shower and bathroom facilities. This camp is on the banks of the Chobe River, and there is great game viewing from camp.

The Kalahari Camp is a permanent lodge with hunting chalets that is located in a dry riverbed and overlooks a water hole frequented by game. Fly camps are often done from this main camp for the hunting of lions. Hunters will spend two to four days at a time in these fly camps. The Central Mountain Camp is a luxurious lodge nestled in the mountains with incredible views over vast stretches of savanna that hold plenty of wildlife. The Northern Camp is still in the planning phase but will be a luxury tented camp (permanent).

All camps have at least four sleeping units with king-size beds and en-suite facilities.

Gerrit Utz: On our ranch, we have four comfortable double rooms with en-suite bathrooms. Every room has its own rifle safe. Just next to the guest rooms there is an entertainment area with seating, a sun umbrella, and a refreshing pool. The farmhouse serves as "base," with all meals taken together in our dining room. Electricity is available twenty-four hours a day for charging camera gear and so on. Guest rooms are serviced on a daily basis.

What to Expect

In our concession area, we have two comfortable safari tents that can hold two hunters each, both with en-suite bathroom and hot and cold running water. The eating area and open fireplace are a short walk away; we eat breakfast and dinner close to the fireplace. All meals are freshly prepared and cooked on the open fireplace. The bush kitchen is equipped with a freezer and many cooling facilities; all drinks and food are stored safely and hygienically.

John Wambach: We offer several camps and options. We have our luxury lodge, with a mountain chalet and luxury tents. We also have a permanent tented camp, which is a bit more rustic. We offer full backpack hunts, and for those we stay in a spike camp in the mountains.

 ## What does a client eat on safari?

Janneman Brand: The client will be eating a lot of venison dishes—kudu steak, springbok osso buco, and oryx schnitzel, to name a few. We also serve freshly baked breads and decadent desserts.

Dirk de Bod: Traditional Namibian meals and barbecue with all kinds of game meat shot by the client.

Kai-Uwe Denker: We serve mainly game meat and, if possible, fresh vegetables. During the day, while we are hunting, we take along a bag with sandwiches, oranges, and water for a cold lunch.

Peter Kibble: We serve a variety of game meat, chicken, pork with vegetables, and salads, all prepared by our trained cook. Some nights we barbecue. All meals are followed by mouthwatering desserts and accompanied by fine South African wines.

Johan Kotzé: We'll have a Continental breakfast: eggs, bacon, fruit, yogurt, and cereals. Lunch will be something light, like meat dishes with salads. Dinner is usually a three-course meal with starter and dessert. We use the meat from the trophies the clients shoot so you will get to taste a variety of African animals. The meat will be served with a variety of other traditional dishes.

Corne Kruger: We eat game meat, and some of the best local food prepared with an international twist by Elsada Kruger.

Joof Lamprecht: Hunters Namibia offers world-class local cuisine expertly prepared by our gourmet chefs and the dedicated kitchen teams. Venison from the hunt is always served accompanied by a wide variety of organically grown

Chalets at the beautifully landscaped KumKum Game Lodge in southern Namibia. (Photo courtesy of Willem Mans)

salads, fruit, vegetables, and herbs from the gardens. Fresh bread, biscuits, and treats are baked daily in the old-fashioned wood-burning oven. Nonvenison as well as vegetarian meals are prepared, with pleasure, on request.

Guests at Lake Lodge may often opt for a picnic-style lunch in the veld and a brief "bush-siesta" in the shade of the majestic acacias, before continuing with the afternoon hunt.

Willem Mans: We serve mostly meat and steaks from the trophies the client has taken.

Diethelm Metzger: For breakfast, we serve cereals, juices, tea or coffee, yogurt, fruit, cold cuts, jams, breads or toast, and scrambled eggs.

Lunch generally consists of sandwiches in the field, which will be prepared by each hunter himself out of the cool boxes. Lunch will be served out in the bush, or in a blind or underneath a nice tree, *Out of Africa*–style. The lunch boxes are stocked with a variety of foods to cater to everyone's taste.

What to Expect

Our dinners are home-cooked meals. We serve game dishes mainly; we try to serve the meat of the animals the hunters have shot themselves. With the meat dishes, which will vary from schnitzel to stroganoff and game steaks, we always serve fresh vegetables, salads, as well as potatoes, rice/pasta, or breads.

Peter Thormählen: This depends totally on the client's preferences. Our clients complete a questionnaire of their food preferences, and we cook what they select!

Jamy Traut: Clients are asked beforehand to indicate their preferred foods and drinks. Most prefer to dine on game they have hunted, but that can be varied with almost anything they want.

Gerrit Utz: On the ranch hunts, here is an example of what we will eat on a normal day:

Breakfast: coffee, tea, cereal selection, yogurt, freshly baked bread, cold cuts, cheese selection, jam selection, honey, and peanut butter or, if the client wishes, eggs, bacon, sausage, etc.

Lunch: Often steaks topped with fried onions or pineapple, potatoes, pasta, rice, different vegetables, salads, and gravy. Dessert is fruit salad or pudding.

Afternoon tea: coffee, tea, and biscuits or cake.

Dinner: Freshly baked bread, cold-cut selection, cheese selection, salad (bean or tomato or carrot salad etc.), fried boerewors or quiche or pasta bake, etc.

On the concession hunts, breakfast will consist of coffee, tea, cereal selection, yogurt, freshly baked bread, cold cuts, cheese, jam, honey, and peanut butter or, if the client wishes, eggs, bacon, sausage, etc. For lunch, we have lunch boxes with us with sausages, cheese, bread, some cooked or fried meat, and vegetables. Additionally we have some fresh fruit and biscuits. For dinner, on the open fire we fry/cook meat dishes with vegetables and potatoes, rice, or pasta together with a salad. Dessert is pudding, fruit salad, etc.

John Wambach: We eat the meat we have killed and offer it with salads, rice, and pastas.

 ## How much walking will a hunter typically do?

Janneman Brand: Between one and five miles a day.

Dirk de Bod: Two to four miles per day for plains game, and five to fifteen for dangerous game.

Ask the Namibian Guides

Kai-Uwe Denker: A lot. It is very difficult to estimate the distance you actually cover when tracking game laboriously over rough terrain. Therefore, it might be more valuable to know that a tough day after elephant means ten hours of walking. On an average day we walk six hours. On a plains game hunt we normally rest over midday. A typical day means two to three hours of walking in the morning and the same in the afternoon.

Peter Kibble: We do not believe in walking a client to death, but some days you could walk two to four miles, depending on the situation.

Johan Kotzé: This is difficult to say. It may be anything from one to five miles a day, I would say. Every day is different, and the weather conditions also play an important role in this. But we won't be walking from sunrise until sunset! We do a lot of driving to get to certain areas, and then stalk to get to the animals.

Corne Kruger: On average, a client will walk about three to four miles a day on a plains-game hunt.

Joof Lamprecht: We use fully equipped Land Cruiser trucks to cover ground. Once a trophy is spotted, we stalk it on foot. Depending on the situation, a stalk could be from two hundred yards to several miles. We do not believe in walking our clients to death.

Willem Mans: Most of the time, if you are hunting kudu and mountain zebra, you will walk quite a lot; the other species require a lot less.

Diethelm Metzger: Depending on the physical ability of the hunter, we shall walk as much as he enjoys. We try to minimize driving around in the hunting vehicles.

Peter Thormählen: I am proud to say that in our company, we DO NOT shoot from hunting vehicles. We hunt in communal concessions in Namibia where shooting from vehicles is NOT allowed. Our clients stalk all their game on foot after it is spotted from the vehicle.

Jamy Traut: This depends very much on the species in question, and also on the fitness of the hunter. Elephant, eland, and buffalo hunting usually require covering quite a bit of ground on foot. However, walking is adjusted as far as possible to the capabilities of the client, which we discuss with the client beforehand. On general plains-game hunts, most of the time is spent traveling in a hunting vehicle, spotting game, and thereafter taking short stalks to get close to potential trophy animals.

If I had to put a mileage on it, I'd say five to ten miles a day on eland and buffalo and double that for elephant. For plains game, although a lot of time is spent on foot, actual distance covered per day is probably only three to five miles.

Gerrit Utz: This very much depends on the general physical condition of the hunter. I like to say that I match or adapt my hunting style to the hunter and not the other way around. If a hunter enjoys walking, we will do a lot of walking and stalking during the hunt.

We do more walking in the concession than at the ranch, as the terrain is very hilly and there are not many roads.

John Wambach: Three to five miles per day is about the average for a lodge or tented camp hunt. A backpack hunt will have you doing about five to ten miles a day.

 ## Are your hunts appropriate for kids/families? How about people with disabilities?

Janneman Brand: Kalahari Safari accommodates many families. In fact, we believe that is our niche in the market—offering personalized family hunting safaris to the discerning hunter.

Dirk de Bod: Family safaris are one of our specialties. Unfortunately, we can't take people with disabilities unless arranged by special request ahead of time.

Kai-Uwe Denker: Kids and families are welcome if they can keep themselves occupied, but there is no extra program for observers or family. Often, if spouses are in good condition, they go along on the hunt.

If the disability is to an extent where the person cannot walk, our camps are not appropriate.

Peter Kibble: We do accommodate families with youngsters on our safaris, and, yes, we can organize a hunt for and accommodate a disabled person.

Johan Kotzé: Yes, families and kids can drive with the hunter during the day. We see so many animals during the day that it is really a "photographic safari" as well! We have a swimming pool at the camp that comes in handy during the hot parts of the day. We can accommodate people with disabilities; the terrain is easy to move around on and also the lodge and the rooms are disability-friendly.

Nonhunting companions who come along on hunts at Makadi Safaris may choose to lounge by the pool during the day. (Photo courtesy of Diethelm Metzger)

Corne Kruger: We specialize in family safaris, and we do also cater to people with disabilities.

Joof Lamprecht: We specialize in family safaris as we believe that "If you take your children hunting, you don't have to go hunting for them." People with disabilities are welcome, and they are specially catered for to enable them to have a successful safari.

Willem Mans: Yes, our hunts are very appropriate for families. We can accommodate disabled persons by waiting at strategic points for game and sometimes shooting from the vehicle.

Diethelm Metzger: Yes, families are very welcome to join the hunters. Kids are also fine, but they should be age eight and above. We have handled people with disabilities before; it can be done.

Peter Thormählen: We specialize in family safaris as we are a close family ourselves. I like children, and my wife, Anso, and I have three children. Our professional hunters are all family-oriented, very well mannered with high family values, and very considerate of children on safari. None of our professional

What to Expect

hunters, including myself, uses any alcohol on safari, tells dirty jokes, or would ever swear in front of a client's wife or children—and we mostly cater to families with children on safari. This is something I am very strict about, and I am proud that our professional hunters are all of a very high class.

We haven't yet had any handicapped hunters on safari, so this is something I have no experience with.

Jamy Traut: We think of our operation as specializing in family safaris. We like to accommodate the whole family and get the youth involved in all aspects of the outdoors (not only hunting). The plains-game areas are suited for handling people with disabilities, but in the Caprivi big-game areas, although it is possible, it will be complicated.

Gerrit Utz: If the children are very small, three to six years old, they can stay at the ranch during the day and play with our children. They would be looked after while dad enjoys some hunting during the day.

People with disabilities will not be able to make a hunt in Damaraland. The terrain is just too difficult, and our facilities at the concession are not suitable for disabled people. It is very stony, and the tents and bathrooms are not built for wheelchair access. On the farm it would be more doable,

Dinners on safari are often gourmet affairs featuring wild game dishes. (Photo courtesy of Diethelm Metzger)

but again, our showers, toilets, and so on are not built for disabled persons. Up to this point in my career, I have not had any inquiries about hunts from disabled persons.

Also have I not yet had a family who went on a hunting trip whose children were not interested in the hunting. On all of the family safaris I've had to the present, the kids always wanted to hunt some small animals, and they joined dad most days of the hunting safari.

John Wambach: We cater to families many times a year and we have many choices of activities to keep everybody happy. We can accommodate hunters with disabilities in some of our camps.

 Is there anything for a nonhunting spouse or companion to do?

Janneman Brand: Nonhunters enjoy accompanying the hunter on his/her quest. Most of our hunters bring their nonhunting wives (because of the luxury accommodations and safe environment), and they enjoy the experience with their spouse. There are many photographic opportunities. A shopping trip to Windhoek can be arranged, and we are building a bush spa to further enhance the experience. As you will be the only hunters in camp, we are flexible and willing to accommodate any special needs or wishes.

Dirk de Bod: We offer game-viewing trips as well as day trips to town with all kinds of shopping.

Kai-Uwe Denker: No. If the spouse or companion wants to come along, she must be aware that she will have to keep herself occupied.

Peter Kibble: Yes, we do arrange sightseeing safaris.

Johan Kotzé: They can join us on the hunt since, as I mentioned, we see a lot of animals during the day while we're driving around. We can also arrange for them to go to Windhoek for a day of shopping. There is a swimming pool at the camp. We also have a water hole in front of the lodge where plenty of animals come to drink during the day.

Corne Kruger: Yes, lots of things! We have a heated pool at the lodge, and Windhoek is only forty-five minutes from camp for shopping trips. There are also many great photo opportunities.

Joof Lamprecht: We find that nonhunting spouses enjoy the safari as much as the hunter because we do not just hunt. We stop to show and explain

What to Expect

Dinner is served on the patio, near a crackling campfire, at Makadi Safaris' Ilala Game Reserve. (Photo courtesy of Diethelm Metzger)

in great detail the fauna and flora to our guests. A photo opportunity is never passed up. We have to send a vehicle to the city of Windhoek every week for supplies, and spouses often accompany Marina on these excursions for some shopping. We will also arrange, on request, for nonhunters to go on tours of Namibia, which we guide ourselves most of the time.

Willem Mans: Apart from observing the hunt, nonhunting clients enjoy walks around the camp area and chatting with my wife, Marita.

Diethelm Metzger: Yes. Bird watching, nature walks, swimming, sunbathing by a very nice swimming pool, and shopping in Windhoek.

Peter Thormählen: There are lots of things to do. We arrange tours for the nonhunting companions if they prefer to tour while their partners are hunting. These tours could be daylong or even last for a couple of days depending on where the hunt is.

Jamy Traut: There is plenty for nonhunters to do in all of our areas. Activities revolve mostly around game viewing, hiking, and trips to national parks and other places of interest. In the Caprivi, game viewing in Chobe National Park and visits to nearby Victoria Falls (which has activities like elephant-back riding) are very popular. All of our permanent camps have swimming or plunge pools and library areas, as well as game-viewing areas overlooking water holes.

Gerrit Utz: An entertainment program is not offered as such. Possibilities are there, such as separate game drives for photography, horseback riding, or day trips to other destinations during a farm hunt. These can keep a spouse or companion busy for a while but not during the whole safari. If the nonhunter likes relaxing and reading at the pool, that would be another option.

On the concession hunts, the companion will have the best time if that person has some interest in hunting and can join us for most of the time during a hunt.

John Wambach: Yes, definitely. There is sightseeing, visiting game parks, touring the Skeleton Coast, being pampered in a spa, horseback riding, stargazing, hot-air ballooning, and shopping for curios.

 ## What's the weather like?

Janneman Brand: The sun always shines in the Kalahari! We have great hunting weather with cold early mornings and evenings, but warm days. We suggest that clients layer their clothing so they can take clothes off as the day warms up.

Dirk de Bod: The weather in Namibia is usually sunny 300 days of the year. Rain falls mainly in the summer months, from November to March. In fall (March to mid-May), it ranges from 75 degrees F at night to 105 midday. In winter, (mid-May to mid-August), it can be 30 degrees at night and 75 degrees midday. In spring (mid-August through November), expect 75-degree temperatures at night and 105 midday.

Kai-Uwe Denker: Mostly dry, sunny weather, very hot in the summer months, and it can be very cold in the mornings and at night in the winter months. We might sometimes have downpours in the rainy season (when we normally don't hunt).

Peter Kibble: In winter it is cold to extremely cold, but acceptable. Summer is hot to very hot but cool in the evenings and very pleasant.

Johan Kotzé: Our hunting season is from 1 February to 30 November. November through March is the rainy season, and it can be very hot then, with thunderstorms. The best time to visit is in the cool, dry winter months,

A relatively unusual sight in Namibia for most of the hunting season: cloud cover. (Photo courtesy of Diethelm Metzger)

May through August, and even into September. In the summer months the daytime temperatures are above 30 degrees Celsius (86 degrees F); nights are cooler. During the winter months, daytime temperatures are in the mid-20s (mid-70s F), but the temperature can go down to freezing in the nights and early mornings.

Corne Kruger: It depends on the season; temperatures can run from 25 degrees F to 120 degrees F in the summer.

Joof Lamprecht: Namibia has 365 days of sunshine. June and July occasionally bring a few days that are bitterly cold—as low as minus 10 degrees Celsius (14 degrees F). December and January are midsummer, and no hunting is allowed. During the rest of the year, the temperature varies between 20 and 30 degrees Celsius (68 to 86 degrees F). Rain rarely interrupts hunting, as thunderstorms mostly last only ten minutes, after which hunting can continue.

Willem Mans: Most hunting is done from April to September, which are the cooler months. Although the occasional cold front can roll in from the cold Benguela current in the Atlantic Ocean and take temperatures down a lot (hardly ever freezing, though), average daily temperatures are around 20 degrees Celsius (about 70 degrees F). With the sun shining most of the time, it is very pleasant from about 10 A.M. to about 4 P.M. even in midwinter.

Diethelm Metzger: Cool mornings and evenings. Warm days. No rain in winter. Usually clear blue skies. Temperatures vary between 10 degrees F and 65 degrees F during the day. In the summer, temperatures may rise to 95 degrees F.

Peter Thormählen: In winter, it is cold at night and in the early morning. In summer, it is hot during the day and cool at night.

Jamy Traut: During most of the hunting season, we have clear skies and cool evenings and mornings. It is hot (80 to 95 degrees F) between 11:00 A.M. and 2:30 P.M., and that is usually the time to take a siesta, for most game is inactive (and difficult to approach). The most popular hunting times are May to August when the field is dry and game viewing is at its best. During June and July, nights can be cold—freezing—but it heats up quickly during the day.

Gerrit Utz: December to April (our summer) is normally our rainy season. It is not that we have day after day of rain, but the clouds build up in late morning, and in the early afternoon it rains. Most of the time, by sunset, we have a clear sky again. This happens on average three times a week, but often it skips one or two weeks. The temperature can go up to 110 degrees F, and it stays warm during the night.

Around 10 May, the temperature goes down close to the freezing point and then the kudu breeding season starts. During the daytime it still gets warm, (90 degrees F), but during the night it can go down to the freezing point. In June and July come cold fronts from the south, and the temperature drops down below freezing.

In August and September it gets warmer again, but the first water ponds start to dry up, since the last water they got was sometime in March or April.

October and November are normally hot, but every year during those two months for a couple of days it gets windy and cold.

John Wambach: We have cool mornings and evenings. Midday can be hot to very hot.

Hard to believe this is a tent! Comfortable, semipermanent accommodations are the norm in Namibia, even in many wilderness areas. (Photo courtesy of Peter Thormählen)

 ## What happens to the meat of the animals your clients shoot?

Janneman Brand: All meat is processed and distributed to the families on the ranch. Nothing goes to waste!

Dirk de Bod: We use as much meat as possible in camp and give some of it to staff, and we donate the rest to schools and the needy.

Kai-Uwe Denker: In the communal concession areas, the meat is distributed to the local community. On private land the meat is either consumed or sold.

Peter Kibble: The meat belongs to the concession owner. If we require meat, we purchase the game meat from him.

Johan Kotzé: We use the meat in camp to feed the clients and give to the staff. A lot of the meat also gets sold to local butchers.

Corne Kruger: We sell most of it, but we also donate meat to the Meals on Wheels organization.

Joof Lamprecht: In camp we serve mostly choice meat from the hunt. Our staff of twenty members consume quite a bit of it. The remaining marketable meat is sold to meat packers for local and export sale.

Willem Mans: We regularly give some to the school hostel at Warmbad and the old-age home in Karasburg. The rest is eaten by us, the hunters and staff, and processed into jerky, sausage, chili bites, etc., to sell later to help cover costs.

Many hunts in Namibia are fun for all ages. Here, twelve-year-old Michael Sherwood poses with his 44½-inch gemsbok taken with Willem Mans in 2010. (Photo courtesy of Willem Mans)

Diethelm Metzger: We serve the meat to our guests. Our staff gets regular rations of meat. Katja processes much of the meat and makes it into sausage, biltong, and smoked meat. If we have more meat than we can handle, we will sell it to a meat processor in town.

Peter Thormählen: On private properties it remains the property of the owners, who sell the meat to butchers. On the communal concession area, we have to deliver the meat to the different villages for consumption. The people who live in the communal concession area are very poor and they appreciate the meat a lot.

Jamy Traut: We always keep the best cuts for the kitchen. We also support an orphanage in the north that feeds seven hundred children per day. A substantial portion of the meat we hunt goes to that orphanage. The rest of the meat is sold to local butchers.

Gerrit Utz: We use a lot of meat on the ranch for ourselves and the staff working for us. The remaining gets sold to the local butcher.

In the concession, all meat goes back to the community. I am responsible for bringing all the hunted meat to the head office of the conservancy. Even if we shoot an animal far off the road, we have to slaughter it and carry all of the meat out. The conservancy has people who distribute the meat to the people of the community so that everybody gets some meat during the season.

John Wambach: We use as much of it as possible in our camps, and the rest goes toward staff rations.

Hunting Areas in Namibia

Chapter 9

 Describe the area(s) you hunt and tell what makes them special.

Janneman Brand: Kalahari Safari is situated on 35,000 acres of privately owned land in the Kalahari, only two hours' drive southeast of Windhoek International Airport. It is true camelthorn and yellow oak savanna. Surrounding our hunting land, we have 200,000-plus additional acres on which we can hunt, due to hunting agreements with neighboring farmers. The Kalahari is known for the exceptional quality of its gemsbok, springbok, and red hartebeest.

Dirk de Bod: Our main game reserve is located an hour north of the Hosea Kutako International Airport and consists of 48,500 acres of plains and

Namibia's desert regions are truly spectacular. (Photo courtesy of Jofie Lamprecht)

rolling hills. In addition, we have concessions to the north and west that give us access to more than 1.3 million acres of hunting conservancies.

Kai-Uwe Denker: Our big-game concession in northeastern Namibia is especially renowned for big elephant trophies. The terrain in this area is flat, monotonous bushveld with huge baobab trees. Our other hunting area, within the Namibian escarpment, is made special by its spectacular, arid scenery.

Peter Kibble: Our hunting areas range from savanna plains to undulating rolling country with dry riverbeds to mountains and valleys and lovely wooded areas, which gives you the best of everything.

Johan Kotzé: We are on the edge of the Kalahari Desert. The terrain is Kalahari savanna—red sand and grassy plains with big camelthorn trees. The terrain is easy to hunt in and very scenic.

Corne Kruger: Our main area, Omujeve, is in the beautiful hills of central Namibia. We also hunt on the wide-open plains of southern Namibia, in an area called Schonbrunn. This is exciting hunting in an area densely populated with oryx and springbok, with miles of nonperennial rivers in which to stalk. We also have a 400,000-acre free-range concession, Omatendeka, in northwestern Namibia. This is remote, wild, untouched country of mountains and plains.

Joof Lamprecht: The hunting area is privately owned by the Lamprechts and covers an area of over 50,000 acres (approximately 80 square miles) of pristine wilderness, populated only by free-ranging game. The area consists of small rocky hills, vast grassland savannas, and some heavily wooded and bushy areas.

An adjoining property adds another 40 square miles to our hunting area. Twenty-seven species of huntable game, as well as an impressive variety of game birds (depending on the season) are available for trophy hunters and wingshooting enthusiasts. Many additional species can be viewed and photographed. A minimum of 500 game animals will be seen in one day while hunting.

The hunting areas are either the Lamprechts' privately owned Rooikraal and surrounding concessions (for classic plains-game safaris), or the exclusive Waterberg Plateau Park concession—all pristine wilderness, populated only by free-ranging dangerous game. The Waterberg has not been hunted for eight seasons; the trophy quality is, therefore, superb.

The elevation of our property and concession is almost 2,000 meters (6,562 feet) above sea level.

Willem Mans: We hunt mainly in the 50,000-acre unspoiled KumKum Game Ranch, which is our base and which holds a wide array of good African game. There is also an abundance of fish in the Orange River in this region as well.

A view of the Namibian escarpment. (Photo courtesy of Kai-Uwe Denker)

Hunting Areas in Namibia

Diethelm Metzger: Makadi's main hunting area on Neu-Otjisauona and Zwerveling consists of camelthorn savanna and open and flat grassland in the south; there is an abundance of red hartebeests, Burchell zebras, springboks, and warthogs in this area. Then we have rolling hills with several *omurambas*—dry riverbeds overgrown with high grasses—forming a beautiful landscape and supplying much water during the rainy season. Hilltops are brushy. This is where kudus, elands, and gemsboks are mostly found. Riverbeds and dams are home to waterbucks and duikers. The very northern parts of the hunting area are rocky and mountainous.

On Schoengelegen, we have beautiful vistas and very rocky terrain. Very good kudus are found here, as well as hartebeests, gemsboks, and warthogs.

The Otjihaenena area is relatively flat with quite a bit of bush. This makes for easy walking. Here we hunt for gemsboks, hartebeests, kudus, warthogs, steenboks, and duikers.

The Omitara area is open and flat, some bush with hills in between, mainly camelthorn savanna. This is a good area for springboks and kudus.

The Claratal area is west of Windhoek. It consists of rolling hills and beautiful scenery. This is where we hunt springboks and mountain zebras.

The Ilala Private Game Reserve is probably the most exhilarating area available. Situated close to the Namib Desert, it has rugged mountains, rough terrain, and desert, but also beautiful vistas. The reserve is home to large kudus, gemsboks, springboks, klipspringers, hyenas, and beautiful mountain zebras. It is here where we conduct our leopard hunts.

Peter Thormählen: One of the areas we hunt is in the central Kalahari Desert. The beauty of the central Kalahari, with its huge camelthorn trees, white grass, and red dunes make this an unforgettable experience! There is no way to describe the beauty of the Kalahari unless you have seen the sun come up as a huge red ball in the morning and experienced the spectacular Kalahari sunsets. The beauty of this Namibian region is not copied anywhere else in Africa!

Our Kaokoland concession is equally spectacular. Huge granite mountains towering over broad plains with white grass in winter and dry riverbeds with huge acacia trees make for another unforgettable safari. The combination of granite boulders, mopane tree clusters, huge mountains, and spectacular plains with gemsboks, springboks, and mountain zebras fascinates our clients with its beauty and special romance. Traveling here requires covering huge distances, as the concession is unfenced and covers 495,000 acres.

Namibia is famous for its excellent populations of gemsbok. (Photo courtesy of Diethelm Metzger)

Jamy Traut: Our Caprivi area consists of mostly flood plains with tree islands, which we hunt from a boat and on foot. It is very pretty hunting country where probably more elephants are seen per day than in any other Namibia concession. It is not uncommon to see 250 to 400 elephants per day during the dry season. The waterways make this area special, but they also make it difficult to hunt at times; consequently, hunters always feel they have achieved something special when they successfully take their game.

Our Kalahari Game Lodge is an 80,000-acre area of typical Kalahari dunes and grasslands with big pans (dried-out water holes) and big camelthorn trees. This beautiful semidesert region contains large numbers of game indigenous to this area, including a healthy lion population.

Our Central Camp is part of the 200,000-acre Dordabis Conservancy. This area is typical savanna grassland with thorn-tree islands and plenty of small mountains. To the west, these mountains and canyons become more pronounced. The variety of game here is incredible.

Hunting Areas in Namibia

Gerrit Utz: Damaraland, where our concession is located, is probably one of the prettiest parts of Namibia, maybe even the nicest. The animals and the area call to mind the early days of Africa; the antelopes move freely between the elephants and lions. Humans have not yet disturbed and commercialized much of the natural world, and it remains as it was a hundred years ago.

On our ranch, we try to keep the area open and natural for the game, as much as possible. We try to build habitats that are appropriate for the game species living here, and we try to show the hunter a piece of Africa that is as wild and natural as is possible on a commercial ranch.

John Wambach: We hunt where the game species occur naturally, and therefore our clients will be hunting in several different areas on one safari. We specialize in mountain hunts in totally free-range and unfenced regions. We hunt in the flat savannas and bushveld as well. Hunting in an area where the species occurs naturally gives a hunter the best chance of getting a good trophy and of enjoying the best hunt for that particular species, as it is king in its area.

 What section of the country is your area(s) in?

Janneman Brand: We are located in Namibia's southeast, in the Kalahari Desert.

Dirk de Bod: The main game reserve is located 60 miles north of the Hosea Kutako International Airport in Windhoek. We also have a Northwest Camp 100 miles to the west and a Far North Camp 220 miles to the north.

Kai-Uwe Denker: The big-game area is in the northeast along the Botswana border to the south of Khaudum Game Park, and the second area is in northwestern Namibia within the escarpment.

Peter Kibble: We hunt in areas mostly east of Windhoek, the capital city of Namibia.

Johan Kotzé: Our area is in southeastern Namibia, about 112 miles from Windhoek.

Corne Kruger: Our main area is in the beautiful hills of central Namibia, just 37 miles from the airport. We have another area, Schonbrunn, in southern Namibia. We also have a 400,000-acre free-range concession in northwestern Namibia.

Ask the Namibian Guides

Greater kudu are extremely wary and never easy to hunt. (Photo courtesy of Diethelm Metzger)

Joof Lamprecht: Our property is situated one hour by road east of the capital, Windhoek, and a thirty-minute drive from the international airport.

Willem Mans: We are located in the deep south, in the Orange River area.

Diethelm Metzger: Our areas are in the central highlands, 81 miles northeast of Windhoek. Ilala Game Reserve is situated to the west, close to the Namib Desert.

Peter Thormählen: One area is in the central Kalahari; the other is in northern Kaokoland, bordering the Etosha National Park on the west.

Jamy Traut: Our Caprivi area is in the Caprivi Strip, in the northeast. The northern sandveld area is in the tropical Kalahari 100 miles east of Etosha National Park. The Dordabis Conservancy is 100 miles east of Windhoek, and the Kalahari Game Lodge is in southern Namibia, bordering Kalahari Gemsbok National Park.

Hunting Areas in Namibia

Gerrit Utz: The ranch is northeast of Windhoek. Driving time from the airport is one and a half hours and from Windhoek, two hours.

The concession borders the southwestern corner of the Etosha National Park. Distance from Windhoek to the concession is 360 miles. Driving time from airport to camp is nine hours.

John Wambach: We have areas in the central, western, northern, and eastern part of Namibia.

 Describe the type of game available in your area(s).

Janneman Brand: We have eighteen plains-game species. As mentioned, the Kalahari is best known for gemsbok (oryx), springbok, and red hartebeest. As we only take one hunting group at a time and only a limited amount of hunters per year, the quality of our game is very high.

Dirk de Bod: We offer thirty-one species in our various areas, including black wildebeest, black-faced impala, blesbok, blue wildebeest, Damara dik-dik, duiker, Cape and Livingstone eland, gemsbok, hartebeest, impala, klipspringer, kudu, lechwe, leopard, nyala, roan, sable, springbok, tsessebe, waterbuck, and plains and mountain zebra.

Kai-Uwe Denker: In the northeast we hunt elephant, leopard, roan, eland, kudu, blue wildebeest, hyena, hartebeest, gemsbok, springbok, warthog, common duiker, and steenbok. In the northwest, we hunt greater kudu, gemsbok, Hartmann zebra, black-faced impala, springbok, and klipspringer.

Peter Kibble: Hartmann mountain zebra, Burchell zebra, red hartebeest, gemsbok, southern impala, springbok, duiker, steenbok, southern greater kudu, warthog, waterbuck, sable, giraffe, black rhino (property of the state), brindled or blue wildebeest, black wildebeest, klipspringer, leopard, cheetah, baboon, and jackal.

Johan Kotzé: The Kalahari is known for its springbok and oryx. We also have steenbok, duiker, warthog, blesbok, impala, kudu, hartebeest, blue wildebeest, black wildebeest, waterbuck, zebra, giraffe, eland, and sable.

Corne Kruger: Among our various areas, we hunt all the game that can be found in Namibia, including nyala, sable, and roan.

Joof Lamprecht: Baboon, blesbok, Cape buffalo, cheetah, Damara dik-dik, common duiker, Cape eland, Livingstone eland, giraffe, red hartebeest,

141

Most of Namibia's buffaloes are found in the northern regions of the country. (Photo courtesy of Jofie Lamprecht)

black-faced impala, southern impala, jackal, klipspringer, southern greater kudu, leopard, lynx (caracal), gemsbok, white rhino, southern roan, southern sable, Kalahari springbok, steenbok, warthog, common waterbuck, black wildebeest, blue wildebeest, Burchell zebra, and Hartmann mountain zebra.

Willem Mans: Gemsbok, springbok, kudu, red hartebeest, Hartmann mountain zebra, klipspringer, blesbok, Cape eland, steenbok, ostrich, blue wildebeest, and predators.

Diethelm Metzger: Kudu, gemsbok, hartebeest, springbok, warthog, duiker, steenbok, Hartmann mountain zebra, Burchell zebra, black wildebeest, baboon, and jackal. Upon request, we also hunt blue wildebeest, eland, cheetah, leopard, giraffe, waterbuck, klipspringer, sable, roan, and impala.

Peter Thormählen: In Kaokoland we hunt desert lion, desert leopard, spotted hyena, and cheetah; plains game species on quota are oryx (gemsbok), springbok, Hartmann zebra, southern greater kudu, klipspringer, Cape eland, and steenbok.

In the central Kalahari we hunt black and blue wildebeest, red hartebeest, blesbok, waterbuck, springbok, black-faced impala, southern impala, Cape eland, springbok, Burchell zebra, and southern greater kudu.

Jamy Traut: In the Caprivi Strip we hunt elephant, buffalo, hippo, crocodile, leopard, red lechwe, sitatunga, kudu, warthog, and bushpig.

In the northern sandveld we hunt eland, kudu, Burchell zebra, dik-dik, gemsbok, hartebeest, blue wildebeest, impala, springbok, giraffe, blesbok, steenbok, duiker, warthog, cheetah, leopard, and small cats.

In the Dordabis Conservancy we hunt eland, kudu, Burchell zebra, Hartmann mountain zebra, klipspringer, gemsbok, hartebeest, blue wildebeest, impala, springbok, giraffe, blesbok, steenbok, duiker, warthog, leopard, cheetah, and small cats.

Around the Kalahari Game Lodge, we have lion, eland, gemsbok, springbok, red hartebeest, blue wildebeest, duiker, steenbok, and others.

Gerrit Utz: On the ranch are found eland, kudu, gemsbok, hartebeest, black wildebeest, blue wildebeest, Burchell zebra, Hartmann zebra, springbok, warthog, steenbok, duiker, waterbuck, blesbok, tsessebe, roan, sable, black-faced impala, leopard, cheetah, and giraffe.

In the concession we hunt elephant, lion, spotted hyena, brown hyena, leopard, cheetah, kudu, gemsbok, springbok, klipspringer, Hartmann zebra, ostrich, black-faced impala, steenbok, giraffe, baboon, and jackal.

John Wambach: Mountain zebra, leopard, kudu, oryx, klipspringer, cheetah, blue wildebeest, black wildebeest, red hartebeest, springbok, steenbok, duiker, Damara dik-dik, impala, warthog, and eland.

 ## Describe the topography of your area(s).

Janneman Brand: Savanna landscape with camelthorn trees.

Dirk de Bod: Savanna plains and rolling hills, with acacia trees and indigenous shrubs.

Kai-Uwe Denker: The area in the northeast is flat, monotonous bushveld with huge baobab trees. The area in the northwest consists of steep, rugged mountains going over into undulating desert plains through which a few big, dry watercourses cut.

Peter Kibble: Our hunting areas vary from savanna plains to undulating rolling country with dry riverbeds, to mountains and valleys and lovely wooded areas, which gives you the best of everything.

Johan Kotzé: The topography is mostly flat, grassy plains with large camelthorn trees and a variety of other trees and bushes.

Corne Kruger: A mix of open savannas, rolling hills, and mountains.

Joof Lamprecht: The area consists of small rocky hills, vast grassland savannas, and some heavily wooded and bushy areas.

Willem Mans: A mix of mountains and wide-open plains.

Diethelm Metzger: Rolling hills, open savanna, mountains, dry riverbeds, open grasslands, ponds, and bushveld.

Peter Thormählen: The central Kalahari Desert consists of huge camelthorn trees, white grass, and red dunes. Our Kaokoland concession features huge granite mountains towering over huge plains with white grass in winter and dry riverbeds with huge acacia trees.

Jamy Traut: The Caprivi area has riverine forest and open flood plains (grass). Two rivers, the Kwando and the Chobe, form the borders.

The northern sandveld is tree- and bush-rich country and flat sandveld, with large *manketti*, camelthorn, and marula trees. This is a highly productive area for game.

The Dordabis Conservancy is savanna grassland with hills and mountains.

The Kalahari Game Lodge is situated in an area of red dune grasslands with camelthorn trees.

Hunting Areas in Namibia

A scenic view in Ilala Game Reserve in western Namibia. (Photo courtesy of Diethelm Metzger)

Gerrit Utz: The farm has a bit of everything. In general, the farm is hilly with the northern part covered in bushveld and thornveld. It varies from open bushveld to dense, thick bush. We have many areas with open water for the game. The southern part is hilly with dry riverbeds and some hills. The east consists of big, wide plains and holds the game species that prefer more open country.

In the concession, in the western part, we have a big mountain range with high table mountains. The bush is mostly mopane, and there are many natural springs in that area. In the south is the Huab River (a dry riverbed) with huge ana and camelthorn trees. The riverbed is in a long valley, going right through the concession from east to west. In the east and north, where we do not do much hunting except for elephant and sometimes springbok and giraffe, it is quite flat with rock kopjes. Most of the human population

Namibia's distinctive quiver tree. (Photo courtesy of Diethelm Metzger)

live in that area. The whole area is at least semidesert. The Damaraland region is, in terms of the quality of the landscape, probably the prettiest part of Namibia.

John Wambach: Savanna, bushveld, sandveld, desert, and mountains.

 Describe the ownership of the land(s) you hunt, for example: Is it a privately owned farm or ranch? If you hunt in a concession or conservancy, whether government or communal, explain what that means. Who owns it, and who is allowed to hunt there? How is it different from hunting on a farm or ranch?

Janneman Brand: The 35,000-acre ranch is privately owned land. I am the third generation on the ranch and the entire operation is family owned and run.

Dirk de Bod: We start most safaris at our privately owned game reserve, and we hunt in concession areas to the northwest for other species.

Kai-Uwe Denker: We privately own a 24,000-hectare (59,300-acre) property within the Erongo Mountain Rhino Sanctuary in the Namibian Escarpment.

In the northeast, we hunt in communal conservancy concessions. This means the local community has formed a conservancy with all that implies: A management plan is created, then the appointed committee for the conservancy applies for a hunting quota and sells the hunting rights mostly on a tender basis. If the contract expires and the cooperation between the committee for the conservancy and the concession holder is satisfactory, they might negotiate a new contract for an agreed-on period of time. In the contract, all details of the operation of the hunt, employment of members of the local community, meat distribution, etc., are indicated.

On a farm, the hunting or any other rights and consequently the meat of the hunted game belong to the owner of the farm; in comparison, in the conservancy, the meat belongs to the local community.

Any infrastructure that is constructed in a conservancy or state concession has to be agreed upon with the committee or ministry respectively, and it has to stay there or be removed as required.

Peter Kibble: We hunt mostly on privately owned land in a conservancy area. It is mostly ranchland, but it covers enormous areas with a large high-

A typical hunting area in Namibia, with rolling hills and thornbrush scrub. (Photo courtesy of Diethelm Metzger)

fenced area in excess of 74,131 acres—this gives you fair chase with select hunting rights.

Johan Kotzé: The ranch is privately owned by Namibian partners. I also hunt on other privately owned ground.

Corne Kruger: Most of the areas where we hunt are privately owned, but we also hunt in some conservancies. The conservancies are owned by the local tribes, and they get a quota of game from the government that they then sell to outfitters. We have a ten-year contract with the conservancy we work with; we are the only outfit allowed to hunt in this area during the time specified by the contract.

Joof Lamprecht: The hunting area is privately owned by the Lamprechts.

Willem Mans: We hunt on our own ranch. We also have two concessions with our neighbors, with each about 100,000 acres.

Hunting Areas in Namibia

Diethelm Metzger: Yes, all of it is privately owned ranchland. Neu-Otjisauona, Otjihaenena, and Ilala Private Game reserve are owned by us. They contribute 78,000 acres of available hunting area. Schoengelegen and Zwerveling are 28,000 acres in size. We have the sole hunting rights to those areas, and we are also responsible for the management of the habitat and the populations. We also set the quotas. We have been hunting in the Omitara as well as in the Claratal areas for the past fifteen years. These are also privately owned ranches and are 70,000 acres in size.

Peter Thormählen: The property in the central Kalahari is a privately owned farm. Our Kaokoland area is a communal conservancy owned by the Osiherero people. They own the land, but the Namibian government, under the Ministry of Environment & Tourism (MET), sets the yearly trophy and "own use" quota. The trophy quota consists of the animals we hunt with foreign clients, while the "own use" quota is a MET permit the community applies for in order to hunt animals for their own consumption. The WWF is very involved in the development of the communal conservancies and oversees the quotas set by the MET.

Jamy Traut: The Caprivi Strip area consists of three communal conservancies (Kasika, Impalila, and Kwandu). These are government owned, but the local community receives an approved quota of game that they can sell to an outfitter. The northern sandveld, Dordabis Conservancy, and Kalahari Game Lodge are privately owned ranches.

Gerrit Utz: The farm we hunt on has been privately owned by our family since 1982.

Both Damaraland concessions are communal land. The land belongs to the government, but the Ministry of Environment and Tourism awards a yearly hunting quota to the area. The funds derived from hunting in those areas do not flow into government accounts; the community in that conservancy area receives those funds. I have had the sole hunting rights in the #Khoadi //hoas Conservancy since 1999 and the //Huab Conservancy since 2010.

The biggest difference between the farm and the communal conservancies is that on the farm I set my own quotas and deal with everything myself. In the conservancy, meetings are held with the conservancy committee and the decisions are made with the goal of improving the living standard of the local population.

John Wambach: We own our own mountain wilderness area. We also have access to concessions. Government concessions are hunting areas owned

149

Namibia is surprisingly mountainous in many places. Parts of the central region reach elevations of nearly 6,000 feet.

by the government; they are put out on tender and one concessionaire is allowed to hunt on it. A communal conservancy is where the community has been granted a quota of game by the government for the benefit of the members of the community. They will then also tender this and it is awarded to one concessionaire.

 ## Are any of the areas where you hunt high fenced? How large should a fenced area be to ensure fair-chase hunting?

Janneman Brand: Our 35,000-acre area is high fenced. According to Namibian law, this is the only way that we can own the game on the ranch as well as set the prices. Within the high-fenced area, it is all fair-chase hunting. I believe in fair chase and ethical hunting.

Hunting Areas in Namibia

Dirk de Bod: Yes, the private game reserve where we do most of our hunting is high fenced. Fenced areas should be 10,000 acres or larger.

Kai-Uwe Denker: No, we do not hunt in high-fenced areas. If a game animal is not able to escape from hunting pressure by leaving the area—that means crossing over the border and thus retreating irretrievably beyond the hunter's reach—in my opinion, there can be no talk of fair chase.

Peter Kibble: There is a large high-fenced area in excess of 74,131 acres.

Johan Kotzé: Yes, it is high fenced. In high-fenced areas, there is a much larger variety of species. Areas we hunt in are not less than 8,000 acres.

Corne Kruger: Yes, some of our areas are high fenced. I think 5,000 acres is big enough for fair-chase hunting.

Joof Lamprecht: Our 80-square-mile property is high fenced.

Willem Mans: Yes. For fair chase, an area should be 20,000 acres. KumKum, our base, is 50,000 acres. On such a big, mountainous area, you will hardly ever see the fence, but it is high fenced to prevent the disappearance

Namibia is the only country in Africa with a huntable population of cheetah (although they cannot be exported to the United States).

This huge springbok was taken in Damaraland; it currently ranks No. 2 in the SCI record book. Shown with PH Gerrit Utz is his tracker, Jesu. (Photo courtesy of Gerrit Utz)

of expensive animals that were wiped out in the early days and have now been reintroduced. We believe 50,000 acres is as good as free roaming.

We also have concessions with our neighbors—one place is 100,000 acres, also high fenced. Then there is another about 100,000 acres, which is not high fenced.

Diethelm Metzger: Neu-Otjisauona and Zwerveling are part of a conservation area, and because of that they are partly fenced. This conservation area has a total size of 61,000 acres. Of this, Zwerveling and Neu-Otjisauona constitute 36,000 acres. It is difficult to say how big an area must be to allow for fair-chase hunting. It really depends on the species and the habitat, but generally I would think that fair chase with ample cover starts at 5,000 acres.

Peter Thormählen: Our central Kalahari area is high fenced and has low cattle fences as well. In total, the high-fenced property covers 12,500 acres while the low-fenced property is 42,000 acres. I think an area bigger than 10,000 acres can be considered fair-chase hunting.

Jamy Traut: The Caprivi is unfenced. Approximately 50 percent, or 20,000 acres, of the northern sandveld area is high fenced. About 30 percent, or 40,000 acres, of the Dordabis Conservancy is high fenced. All of the 80,000-acre Kalahari Game Lodge is fenced. As long as there are no internal fences, I believe any area of 10,000 acres or larger can be considered "fair chase."

Gerrit Utz: Part of the ranch is high fenced for the rare species. The remaining part together with two neighbors is high fenced, which gives us a total area of about 42,000 acres. Our idea was to protect our common game against the influences from outside, such as high off-takes. We have been very successful with that and have rebuilt a healthy game population as a result.

The part of my area that is high fenced for the rare game is about 5,000 acres. If you hunt in that area and hunt an animal like an eland by tracking, I personally think it is not easy. It sometimes takes a couple of days, and sometimes we are not successful. You have no guarantee that you will find the animal you want. Of course, when you hunt in that area, you will see the fence every now and then. But I believe you still can do good hunts in fenced areas.

The concession area, however, has NO fences. There are some old cattle fences for the domestic animals in some areas, but elephants and zebras have broken most of these. In our main hunting area there are no fences, just wild country.

John Wambach: Yes, due to veterinary requirements some species have to be kept away from cattle, and therefore the areas where they roam are high fenced. A fenced area should not be smaller than 11,000 acres.

Parting Thoughts

Chapter 10

 What do you see for the future of hunting in Namibia?

Janneman Brand: The future of Namibian hunting is in the hands of the outfitters. If we can adhere to lawful and ethical hunting, Namibia will prove itself as the premier African hunting destination.

Dirk de Bod: Hunting in Namibia is growing every year.

Kai-Uwe Denker: The future of hunting in Namibia is dependent on the future of hunting in general. During the last few years, a great amount of work has been done by various organizations and individuals to get the principle of sustainable utilization of wildlife generally accepted and to promote respectful, ethical hunting, so the future of hunting could be bright. However, the most loathsome unethical practices like canned hunting, put-and-take, and so on continue to jeopardize all this good work and threaten the future of hunting. In my opinion, "supermarket hunting" for nonindigenous species behind high fences does the same. Namibia finally has matured into one of Africa's most rewarding destinations. If we can avoid making it a second South Africa, it has a bright future.

Peter Kibble: As long as people want to hunt, there will be a future in hunting.

Johan Kotzé: It will only go from strength to strength. Privately owned farms invest a lot of money in game and accommodations to cater to the wishes of their clients. The wide variety of species on farmland actually makes hunting on farms the biggest contributors to wildlife conservation in this country.

Corne Kruger: The future of hunting depends on the Namibian government and the decisions it makes. At this stage, the industry is growing and the future looks good.

Joof Lamprecht: The hunting industry in Namibia has grown each year by huge percentages. Our country's constitution enshrines the concept of

Parting Thoughts

A lilac-breasted roller. (Photo courtesy of Jofie Lamprecht)

"sustainable utilization of wildlife." Hunting forms a large part of our country's GDP and is totally supported and approved by our government.

Willem Mans: As long as there are hunters, Namibia will have a good hunting future because it offers good quality and affordable hunts in an "out-of-this-world" atmosphere.

Diethelm Metzger: I foresee a great future for hunting in Namibia, given our natural abundance of game and our mostly pristine African landscape. This is based on the assumption, however, that all players behave themselves and do what they are supposed to do. The professional hunter has to live up to his code of conduct and be the guardian of our wildlife; the hunter has to insist on ethical hunting and accept the PH's code of conduct. Finally, since the government is the law-enforcing agent, it should be up to government to see to it that the hunter abides by the rules. If this is secured, we will have an abundance of wildlife for generations to come.

Peter Thormählen: I personally think that Namibia offers huge opportunities for trophy hunting. I do not think that Namibia has utilized more than 25 percent of its hunting potential at the moment. But this is just my personal opinion.

Ask the Namibian Guides

Jamy Traut: Namibia is arguably the country in Africa with the brightest future when it comes to hunting. The reason, mostly, is its political stability, but there is also a general understanding among its people about why wildlife and sustainable utilization is so important.

It also has many untapped hunting resources, and with a little effort, may become one of Africa's leading lion-hunting destinations. Antihunting groups are active in Namibia just as they are all over the world, but with so many Namibians dependent on the country's natural resources and how well we manage them, I believe that sanity will prevail here when the future looks gloomy in many other places.

Gerrit Utz: In comparison to other African countries, we are very lucky to have a government that is very much in favor of tourism and hunting. We are in the fortunate position that we as hunters can talk to our ministry and work with them, even when it comes to changing laws or implementing new laws. That gives us a big advantage over many other African countries. I believe if Namibia goes on like this, there will still be hunting in our country when other countries have stopped hunting.

Our game population is growing; we have many species to hunt; there are species that can be legally hunted only in Namibia; the variety of species we can hunt is growing; what else do we want? Something must be going well in Namibia!

I see a very optimistic future for hunting in Namibia if in five, ten, or twenty years we still can hunt legally in our world.

John Wambach: The future will be good if the authorities can keep rogue operators out of the country, keep the safari operators on track, and keep everything from becoming too commercialized.

How does hunting help the people and wildlife of Namibia?

Janneman Brand: Hunting provides revenue, job opportunities, and food to the local communities. A hunting operation employs many more staff than other types of farms and, thus, provides many more opportunities for the local people. Wildlife is managed and cared for, as it provides income to the farmer and the people.

Dirk de Bod: Hunting provides benefits to the people of Namibia directly from the availability of meat, as well as job creation, good salaries, and a better way of life.

The southern greater kudu is one of Namibia's signature animals. Horns longer than fifty inches are not uncommon. (Photo courtesy of Jofie Lamprecht)

Sociable weaver birds construct their nests on telephone poles as well as in trees. (Photo courtesy of Willem Mans)

Kai-Uwe Denker: If practiced sensitively and sensibly, sustainable, trophy hunting could add tremendously to the welfare of the Namibian population and the conservation of Namibia's nature.

However, serious negative side effects of trophy hunting have to be addressed. Take, for example, the inbreeding of black-faced impala with introduced southern impala. As well, the falsification of Namibia's uniqueness and the disrespect for other countries' specialties have nothing to do with conservation. Kafue lechwe, for example, belong in Zambia, and not in the semidesert.

Peter Kibble: Because there is a price on the game that people come to hunt, the spin-off value is enhanced. Namibia has so much game because of the hunter, and because of the hunter we ensure the survival of our game. This, in turn, helps to feed people and brings wealth to the country in a practical way; many landowners, instead of culling their animals, realize their value.

Parting Thoughts

Johan Kotzé: More jobs are created for the people of Namibia—everything from skinners and trackers to cleaners, laundry personnel, etc. Also, wildlife populations have definitely increased through hunting. This has come about from of the value placed on animals because of hunting.

Corne Kruger: Hunting has put a value on our wildlife, and that is why Namibia has more game than ever. The hunting industry is one of the biggest sources of employment in Namibia today, and the communal conservancies benefit from the income and the meat they receive as a result of hunting. In short, it puts a value on the wildlife, and therefore, people have an economic reason to look after the wildlife.

Joof Lamprecht: A hunting operation employs many more people per operation than does a normal farming operation. Remuneration in the hunting industry is also much higher than in a traditional farming operation. The game population has grown by 100 percent since sustainable utilization began.

Willem Mans: Hunting employs a lot of people and is the best conservation tool for wildlife available. The fact that there is more game outside the national parks in southern Africa today compared to fifty years ago is testimony to that.

Diethelm Metzger: Hunting equips wildlife with a monetary value. If people are the beneficiaries, they will preserve, conserve, and manage wildlife populations. Game meat also contributes to the food chain!

Peter Thormählen: There is an old hunter saying the greenies do not want to hear: We create jobs and we conserve wildlife to be available for our children and grandchildren!

Jamy Traut: This is obvious. Before hunting became such an important source of income for rural communities and farmers, wildlife was considered by most people to be a nuisance. Today it is a great asset. I believe that more and more farmland currently used for livestock will be "given back" to wildlife in the future, as it has the potential to feed the nation, in terms of protein and job creation. Hunting is the main reason for wildlife having attained this great value. Without it, a large proportion of our game will disappear. The saying, "If the game pays, it stays," has never been truer, with such a fast-growing human population worldwide.

Gerrit Utz: Hunting conserves the wildlife. There has never been as much game in this country as there is today. Trophy hunting has given real value to the game animals. In the last fifteen years, many cattle farmers have added game and hunting to their operations, or even stopped cattle ranching altogether.

On hunting ranches, a lot of unskilled people get employment and education in tourism and hunting. A normal ranch does not need so many employees.

In the communal areas, the local population is provided with meat, some of them get employment, and through the funds generated through hunting, the local infrastructure is increased and upgraded. Hunters travel to remote areas where tourists don't normally go, and they spend much more than other tourists.

Also, predators are not killed indiscriminately to safeguard domestic animals; instead, foreign hunters hunt the predators, and the local farmer gets some reimbursement for his lost animals.

John Wambach: We have more game now than we did 150 years ago because it has a value now and has become a tool for fighting poverty in marginal areas. Our natural resources are protected in our constitution and are, therefore, of great importance to us as a nation.

 ## Any parting words for someone considering a safari in Namibia?

Janneman Brand: Ernest Hemingway said: "I never knew of a morning in Africa when I woke and was not happy." I believe this to be true of Africa and especially Namibia. Be prepared for one thing—when you have visited Namibia once, you will not be able to get the red Kalahari sand out of your boots . . . you will want to return!

Dirk de Bod: Namibia is a very safe and beautiful country with friendly, helpful people, and an amazing biodiversity.

Kai-Uwe Denker: I am no car salesman, and therefore find it very difficult to offer wisdom to someone who considers something about which he knows nothing as yet.

Peter Kibble: If you hook up with the right outfitter, you should have a very exciting and memorable safari!

Johan Kotzé: You will not be disappointed in the friendliness of the people, the high standard of the hunting operations, or the beauty of Namibia. And, you won't be disappointed in the quality of the trophies!

Corne Kruger: Namibia is the top plains-game safari country in Africa today, and it's a great family destination. Consider Namibia for your next hunt!

An unforgettable sunset after a memorable safari. (Photo courtesy of Diethelm Metzger)

Joof Lamprecht: You'll never be the same after visiting Namibia. You will feel as if you need to return yesterday.

Willem Mans: You owe it to yourself to do it; you will never regret it.

Diethelm Metzger: Namibia is a country of wide-open spaces. It boasts a wide variety of game, and if you find the right outfitter, you will have a hunt of a lifetime.

Peter Thormählen: I have been in a lot of African countries, and Namibia has no equal. The government is doing an absolutely great job in managing the country. It is safe and beautiful, with huge open, unspoiled hunting areas. What more can you ask for if you love the outdoors, hunting, and nature? Everyone who hunts in Africa has to experience Namibia. It is a country where your soul becomes free, where you can relax, enjoy, and have great memories for when you return to the reality of the rat race!

Jamy Traut: Check the references of your PH or outfitter, and check into the areas you will be hunting. Make sure they are the best areas for what you want to hunt.

Safari hunting is a source of jobs in rural areas where there are few options other than subsistence farming.

Remember that Namibia has a few unique species to be hunted in an extraordinary environment. Don't miss out on a hunt for Hartmann zebra or a true eland hunt on foot, even if these may take more time than other species. Celebrate big trophies, but don't let an obsession with the tape measure ruin your safari for yourself and others.

Gerrit Utz: Namibia is a country you need to see and to experience. Once you have been here, most probably you will come again. Our country is great for every kind of African hunting. See you soon in Namibia!

John Wambach: Come to the land of contrasts, and you will be spoiled for the rest of the world.

Stories from the Safari Guides

Chapter 11

 Share a story about a memorable safari experience.

Janneman Brand: Sharing my clients' hunting experiences are all memorable moments to me. Having a young child shoot his or her first trophy, an elderly man making his long-awaited African dream a reality, a child with a disability fulfilling his or her wish, a husband and wife sharing their first African safari together. . . . I cannot choose only one experience.

Dirk de Bod: This is the story of the shortest and most amazing kudu hunt ever! One late evening not too long ago, I got a phone call. The man on the other end had a very distinguished, high-class English accent. He introduced himself as Jeremy, a gamekeeper on a large English estate.

Dirk de Bod and his English client with an incredible 66½-inch kudu. (Photo courtesy of Dirk de Bod)

He immediately started to tell me all about his African experiences, including multiple kudu hunts all over Africa and three trips to the Central African Republic, where he walked for a total of sixty-three days to get a Lord Derby eland and a bongo. As he continued telling me about his wanderings through Africa, I thought, *It looks like I have a client on my hands who is very picky and very specific about his desire for the ultimate kudu hunt.*

Finally he stopped talking and asked, "Are you still there?"

I said, "Yes. When are you coming over?"

"When do you think is the best time for the opportunity to harvest a sixty-plus-inch kudu?" he asked. "I know you can do it; I see in the record books you've taken quite a few over the sixty-inch mark."

I told him that in May I had an opening from the seventeenth to the end of the month, but I stressed that as in all hunting, I could not promise we would hit the jackpot; all we could do is try.

So the seventeenth came around, and I sat at the airport waiting for the London flight to land, wondering if I would be able to identify him before he identified me. Sure enough, out the door walked a clean-cut English gentleman with a military-style haircut. Jeremy had brought his friend, Chris. We all shook hands, made the formal introductions, and off we went.

"How far?" Jeremy asked.

"Sixty kilometers south, close to Dordabis, in the mountains to a ranch called Bergsig, which means 'Mountain view' in Afrikaans," I replied.

At the lodge, the clients unpacked, had lunch, and then went out and sighted in their rifles. At the range, I suggested they sight the guns one inch high at 100 yards because most shots range from 150 to 200 yards, and for that the guns will be close to dead-on.

My assistant PH, Hanes, and Chris decided to head for the plains, and Jeremy and I decided to carry on along the two-track road into the mountains. After about fifteen minutes of driving on the bumpy road, the tracker, Sakkie, pointed out a thicket a third of the way up the mountain and said, "Kudu, but they all look like cows."

We stopped the truck, took the guns and shooting sticks, and made use of the black hook-thorns for cover in order to close the distance for a better look. You never know: Mr. Gray Ghost might be hiding in there with the cows, doing his famous invisible trick.

One by one, the cows broke cover, looked around nervously, and walked hastily higher and higher up the mountain. We still had good cover, so I put

Client Bob Model with PH Peter Kibble and the buffalo they shot on a memorable safari.
(Photo courtesy of Peter Kibble)

up the shooting sticks as a rest for the binocular. I wanted to look at the cows and just enjoy the moment. The next moment, there he was—out of nowhere, in the open, in all his glory—the Gray Ghost!

My heart leaped out of my chest. I was speechless. It was the best kudu I had ever seen—huge, deep curls with very heavy bases. I was stunned. While I tried unsuccessfully to speak, Jeremy asked in a very polite manner, "May I take him?"

Suddenly my voice returned, and I said, "Shoot or I will!"

Jeremy shot, and I could hear the delayed thump as the kudu was more than 250 yards away and still climbing the mountain.

"Reload and shoot again—aim high," I instructed.

The kudu was hit again but did not change stride. At last, he came to a halt and went down. We were breathing hard and still shaking as we climbed up the mountain. It took us twenty-five minutes of climbing to reach him.

What a sight! I could not believe what I was looking at. It was a magnificent animal, much better than I had thought even when I first saw it.

Jeremy said, "He looks pretty good to me."

I replied, "You won't believe how good!"

167

We propped the kudu up and cleaned him up for the pictures as the light began to fade behind the clouds. The trackers soon reached us, carrying the tools to skin and pack him out. I looked in my backpack and found my old trusty SCI measuring tape. *The moment of truth,* I thought. I knew the kudu would go quite a bit over sixty inches, but how much?

Jeremy helped me, and we followed the rib on the outside of the spiral very carefully and then we ran out of tape at the sixty-inch mark. There was still quite a bit of horn left.

Jeremy started to scream, "Thank you, God!"

We marked the sixty-inch spot and measured the rest to an unbelievable 66½ inches. What a day!

Kai-Uwe Denker: Right now, while I am completing this questionnaire in camp, a safari comes to an end that forever will remain a highlight in my hunting career. Outside, the black, burnt veld shows the first sprinkling of green, and I think you can immediately imagine the smell of the wet earth after the first rains and the deafening noise of the cicadas coming to life again after the long dry season. On the evening of the sixth day of the safari, we had a tremendous thunderstorm in camp. It was as impressive as it was frightening to lie in the tent amid blinding lightning and earth-shaking thunder.

Early the next morning we came onto a huge elephant track quite a distance away from camp, headed in the direction of the downpour. We took up the spoor and eventually came up on an enormous, thick-tusked bull. We positioned ourselves in his path and waited for him. When he was only ten paces away, the client brought down the tusker with a classic frontal brain shot.

Today I had the tusks officially weighed by the game ranger. They weigh 105 and 101 pounds, which makes this the third hundred-pounder taken by a client of mine—this is at a time when hundred-pounders were thought to have disappeared from the African game fields!

Peter Kibble: As you can imagine, there are many stories I could tell you from over the years! To relate a story that is fairly up to date, I would like to talk of a buffalo and elephant safari I did with a longtime client and dear friend, Robert Model, a past president of the Boone and Crockett Club. He is such a pleasure to hunt with because he has a great sense of humor, knows the anatomy of the animals, and has a sound knowledge of firearms and ballistics. I first met Bob on a safari he was doing with my father-in-law, Fred Bartlett, forty years ago in Botswana. How the years fly by!

Anyway, I decided to take Bob up to the Caprivi Strip for our hunt. This was in October 2007, so it was getting pretty hot by then and all the trees and bushes were starting their budding process. I decided we would make our camp just outside the hunting area next to the Popa Falls Rapids on the Kavango River, which is a beautiful spot overlooking the rapids.

After we had set up camp amid the Terminalia trees, my trackers made a fire, and Bob and I sat next to the fire with our good old Scotch and waited for the fire to burn down so that we could use the hot coals to barbecue some meat, which I was marinating in a box.

Meanwhile, Bob and I reminisced about the good old days in Kenya as I was from there and Bob had done several safaris there. He knew and had met several old professional hunters that I also knew, so, of course you can imagine how we laughed as we chatted! We were both starving, so I barbecued the meat as one of the staff cooked up potatoes and vegetables, then we sat down under the stars with a good bottle of red wine and had our dinner.

Next morning we awoke to the sound of the rapids and the call of the white-browed robin-chat and various other birds. We had a light breakfast and packed a cool box with drinks and something to eat along the way. We then proceeded to the hunting area, where I stopped at an old ruin so that Bob could take a couple of shots with his rifles, a .375 H&H made by Paul Jaeger and a .470 NE double made by John Rigby, a sidelock.

We set off, encountering a few small groups of buffaloes and a lot of elephant tracks but nothing worth following. We had, however, seen an abundance of game—sables, Chobe bushbucks, impalas, and some lovely kudus. Along the riverside we saw warthogs, waterbucks, hippos, and crocodiles. By noon we decided to take a break and stop for a rest and have something to eat and drink while the heat subsided.

After our siesta I said to Bob, "I have a feeling we are going to shoot a good buff, Old Boy."

"Sounds jolly good, Old Chap," he replied.

Anyway, as luck would have it, we came to a small valley not far from the swamp when I saw a group of buffaloes. I started glassing them and saw OUR buffalo with a good set of horns and magnificent bosses—my old tracker Paulos agreed with me that this one was IT! So we proceeded after them, Bob with his .375 with 300-grain Swift A-Frames and I with my old Westley Richards.

We had to be careful because at that time of year the wind tends to shift direction from time to time, and, of course, Mr. Buffalo has an extremely good nose. Everything was working out just fine and we managed to get up to some thick bush, and we knew the buffaloes were just on the other side. We waited

Client Bob Model made a perfect brain shot on this magnificent elephant. (Photo courtesy of Peter Kibble)

for a few minutes because I was sure they would walk out into an open patch just in front of us.

Well, my guess was right; they did. There in the middle stood our fine bull, about eighty yards away. I put up the shooting sticks and motioned Bob to bring up his rifle and get the bull in his scope, which he did.

I said to Bob, "The moment he is clear of the others, take him out!"

Sure enough, the buffalo parted and the bull was standing proudly on his own apart from the others. Immediately I said, "Shoot, Old Boy."

It was a perfect shot! Bob was delighted, and I was delighted and relieved all at the same time. Things could not have turned out better. We then called up Lucky, my driver, to bring the vehicle. We quenched our thirst and took several pictures of Bob's fine buffalo. We loaded him up in the back of the Land Cruiser and proceeded back to camp.

On arriving back at camp, we were hot and sweaty but elated with the day's hunt. I suggested to Bob we sit in the river in a pool amongst the rocks to cool off and that we each take a gin and tonic with us.

"Jolly good idea, Old Chap," said Bob.

While we were sitting in our rock pool sipping our gins in just our shorts, Bob asked me, "Isn't this river full of crocodiles?"

"Yes," I replied. "That is why Paulos (my tracker) is sitting on a rock with my rifle—just in case!"

"It would be a hell of a thing if a croc rocked up now, wouldn't it!" said Bob.

"It would be a nuisance because we might spill our gins; however, it's most unlikely something like that will happen."

And we toasted each other on the great hunt we had had, enjoyed our rest in the pool, and then returned to camp. That night we had a lovely dinner with wine and talked of the next day's elephant hunt.

We rose early in the morning, at least for Bob and me. As Glen Cottar used to say, "The animals are out there—what's the rush! One just has to find them."

I decided we would drive along the boundary line between Botswana and Namibia on the southeastern border, and it turned out to be heavy going with a deep sand track for miles. We did see some evidence of elephants about a day old. The bush was quite thick in places and by noon it was very hot. Suddenly, my staff in the back of the Land Cruiser said, "STOP, STOP!"

I thought they had seen a big elephant, judging by their excitement! But they had seen a monkey orange tree, and they love eating monkey oranges. So they jumped out and proceeded to collect as many as they could. We went on and on in a big loop, eventually connecting to the main Katima road. On our way back to camp, we did encounter several elephants but nothing worthwhile. Of course, when hunting elephants, one needs a lot of patience.

Next day we had breakfast, and Lucky came to me and said he had mislaid his binocular and that he remembered hanging it on the back of the hunting car the day before when we stopped to collect monkey oranges. Well, you can imagine I was not amused, but Bob said to me, "Well, we just have to go back there, as we cannot lose his binocular."

So I said, "OK, to hell with it; we will go back."

On the way there, we crossed the tracks of three big bulls, so we decided to follow them. It was a beautiful day and we were walking in a lovely teak woodland where all you could hear was the slight rustle of leaves in the soft breeze and the call of Arnot's chat, a small bird that frequents teak woodlands.

After walking quite some distance, we came across some freshly chewed sticks still wet with saliva from the elephant and not long after we came on really fresh, hot dung. I knew then we were close—the wind was still in our favor, and sure enough, we heard the sound of elephants feeding and breaking branches just ahead.

So I said to Bob, "Let us get up close."

But both elephants had broken tusks, so we left them to carry on feeding. After getting back to the truck, we consumed a fair amount of water before proceeding on to the place of the monkey oranges. We found Lucky's binocular lying in the sand track. We decided to turn around and head back in the direction of the river, thinking just maybe we might find elephant tracks on the way.

We had not backtracked more than a mile when Paulos leaned around the side of the cab and said to me there were two elephant bulls on our right, about six hundred yards away. I immediately stopped, jumped up on the back, and glassed them. One was a shooter, so I beckoned to Bob.

The wind and cover was not the best, with sporadic short trees and bushes. Bob had his .470 NE and I had my faithful Westley. We made a big detour to get the sun and wind in our favor, and by that time it was midafternoon. We made our approach and eventually got within seventy-five feet of the big elephant.

I put up the shooting sticks as I wanted Bob to take a brain shot. The elephant was very slightly quartered away from us, so I told Bob to aim for a spot one fist up from the ear hole and one fist forward toward the eye. On his shot, the elephant's back legs buckled and he went straight down. I knew Bob had made a perfect brain shot. I was so pleased with Bob, and I think he was elated with himself. That night we celebrated.

Next day, with sore heads, we collected several people from the local community to help cut up and skin the elephant. After all, they get all the meat from the trophies taken—those are the rules. This, I must say, was one of the most enjoyable safaris I have had in a long time.

Johan Kotzé: Diana Rupp told this story in the introduction of this book, but one of the most memorable occurrences on a safari happened at Erindi when I was guiding Diana and her husband, Scott, on their first safari. We were glassing from the top of a kopje when I spotted a group of hartebeest bulls, and was able to get Scott on the largest one. Right after he shot that one, I pointed out the second-largest one to Diana. She dropped it with one shot,

Swapping stories at the bar of a safari lodge after the hunt. (Photo courtesy of Diethelm Metzger)

and just like that, they had two really outstanding hartebeests, shot within less than a couple of minutes of each other. They were both excellent trophies, but Scott's was particularly impressive and would have been No. 3 or No. 4 in the SCI records at that time. That was a great day.

Corne Kruger: The past twelve years, since I started hunting professionally, have all been memorable. There are some things that stand out, however. Guiding Craig Boddington and his family was one of my most memorable hunts. But the most amazing hunt ever was about seven years ago, when I was still guiding in Erindi. I guided one of my good friends, Gary Farotte from San Jose, to a 63-inch kudu and a 41-inch gemsbok bull—within 45 minutes of each other!

Joof Lamprecht: J.J. was one of those hunters who was interested in one thing only—to hunt elephant. Annually he came to Africa for a fortnight to hunt these huge pachyderms. It did not bother him at all if he never fired a shot, as he knew the big ivory bearers were thinly sown and just to kill something was not his style.

After hearing of larger-than-normal elephants being taken in Namibia, he wrote to me, as e-mail had not been born yet. He explained his passion for hunting these majestic animals, and he assured me that he would not be upset if he never fired a shot because his minimum target weight was seventy pounds per tusk. He assured me that he knew how rare this size of elephant was.

Later on, in the Caprivi, he told me the story of his previous hunt in a different country, which I will not name. They had spotted a big-bodied jumbo in very thick bush on the edge of a river. After glassing it for what seemed like hours from fairly close, they decided it was worth stalking closer since lush foliage hid the ivory. The elephant would not move. They were so close they could smell the gas emitted by the noisy *blup-blup-blup-blup* of the big bull's flatulence. After an eternity, they decided on a brain shot from about twenty yards. What J.J. did not take into account was the angle of the shot. At this close range, the angle was both very important and very dicey.

After the huge bang from his .505 Gibbs, the bull took off and J.J. waited for the follow-up shot from his PH. No shot. The bull disappeared in the direction of the river. He looked back and saw his PH with a bashful look, staring at him, empty-handed. The PH had left his rifle resting against a tree some twenty yards behind them. They rushed forward and saw the wounded bull climbing up the opposite riverbank, some four hundred yards away . . . into the neighboring country, which they did not dare to enter.

We understood each other straight away, as I would not allow fancy brain shots. "You want to brain-shoot the elephant, you find yourself another PH," I told him.

His rule was simple: He gets to fire the first two rounds, and if the elephant does not go down, I can then drop it. There was no problem. The rules were set and acceptable to all concerned.

On the third day in the western Caprivi we found some fresh tracks about twice my boot length: a possible candidate. We started tracking through the tangled forest. If you have not hunted in this part of the world, I have to explain why I call it a tangled forest.

The Bush people set these areas alight once a year, and the resulting bush fires then rage, out of control, for hundreds of miles. The reason behind this is either to clear the bush in order to plant a crop, as they believe the ashes makes to earth more fertile, or to obtain new green growth, which appears within a few days, that will attract game, which they then can hunt. Well, this tangled mess of fallen trees plus the undergrowth, which is somehow stimulated by the fire, is a tangle of thorns and foliage, and not easy to track or wade through.

After three hours of slogging through this mess, we saw our bull, butt toward us, sleeping in the late-morning heat under an acacia tree. The wind was good, just a slight breeze in our faces. We angled off to the side to try to make out what was in his face. From a distance of about sixty yards we now had a good look at his ivory. J.J. knows elephants and after looking at it for only thirty seconds, he dropped his binocular against his chest and sighed.

The puzzled look on my face asked, "Why the sigh?"

He pulled his shoulders up and two words formed on his lips, "Sixty pounds."

I felt he was being very conservative and concentrated on the bases sticking out of the lips. I was convinced the tusks were quite a bit heavier.

Strange things happen when you stare at something like this for too long; it starts growing and you have to force yourself not to listen to the little devil sitting on your shoulder. I decided to retreat about fifty yards and have a powwow. J.J. remained negative and felt it would be a miracle if it made sixty pounds. I felt confident that it would make the grade.

I've written before to "Trust your PH, as he is the only friend you have right there in a situation like this. If he, however, breaks that trust, you have nothing. So choose your PH carefully."

J.J. decided to go for it. We got into a perfect shooting position about thirty yards away from the bull. He was broadside to us and J.J. had a clear target without any branches in his way. J.J. settled onto the shooting sticks. The air was thick with tension. Suddenly I heard a hiss and looked at J.J. He mouthed the words, "Only one shot."

I smiled and nodded my head. The .505 Gibbs thundered and the bull took off. My .458 struck it perfectly in the root of the tail. It was almost as if somebody pulled up the bull's emergency brake. He sat down right there with a shattered pelvis. J.J.'s shot was perfect and had gone through the top of the heart.

After the insurance shot into the brain, we sent word to the locals that an elephant was down. Within a couple of hours, the bull was being butchered, and that evening the drumbeats could be heard until late. Local bellies were overfull from too much elephant meat.

The next day, we placed the tusks on the scale, and they read 70 and 77 pounds. J.J. was thrilled. He looked at me and said, "Let's go to your place and hunt some plains game. I've shot my last elephant."

I couldn't disagree, for I had done this too many times.

This was to be my last elephant as well.

Willem Mans: My most unforgettable safari was also an unfortunate one. It occurred when a German hunter wounded a leopard at a blind in the early

A beautiful kudu taken with Makadi Safaris. (Photo courtesy of Diethelm Metzger)

evening. We followed the leopard on foot the next morning until it suddenly came charging from an outcropping (kopje) and jumped on the back of my main tracker, who was running away.

Luckily, as the leopard was in the process of jumping onto my tracker, both the hunter and I had hit it well. Our shots thankfully resulted in the leopard rolling over dead just after he landed on the tracker. We rushed the tracker to the local clinic where he received twenty-seven stitches. The leopard's attack lasted less than one second, so it's easy to understand the damage an uncontrolled and wounded leopard can inflict. The tracker is fine to this day.

Diethelm Metzger: Which story do you want to hear? The story of the humble leopard, the story of the gray ghost, the story of my first buffalo hunt, or the story of my quiet hunter from Austin? If you have been in the business for more than twenty years, you surely have many stories to tell. And I can tell stories, but writing them is a totally different cup of tea; nevertheless, I will try my best.

Mom, Dad, and Son had booked a ten-day plains game safari with us. They are a really nice family, and this was actually to be Son's graduation present.

Stories from the Safari Guides

Mom was on vacation, so she read and lounged around the pool and enjoyed gin and tonics.

Dad, Son, and I took off to the shooting range, a standard procedure at Makadi Safaris. First, we discussed shot placement, and I explained why our ideas differ from *The Perfect Shot*. Then, we review safety rules, which is a very important aspect for various reasons. First, I love my life, and I want to enjoy it much longer; I hope the visiting hunter feels this way, too.

Things can happen very fast. I had a friend who died at the age of twenty-four from an accident that shouldn't have happened. A visiting hunter was walking behind my friend when his gun discharged, and my friend was shot in the lower back. Every year hunting accidents happen. I take safety very seriously, and I expect my hunters to respect that.

Therefore, I always stress the importance of never having a round in the chamber when traveling in a hunting vehicle. Never have a round in the chamber when stalking through the bush, either. I always tell the hunter when it is time to chamber a round.

Well, Dad had some questions about getting into a situation where there might not be enough time to put a bullet into the chamber. "Besides," he said, "loading a rifle at that point would be much too noisy."

I replied that there is always enough time. I also said that if you chambered a round quietly, there is no problem. And besides, I told him, if we really missed an opportunity, he wasn't to worry—the next one is around the corner. Dad respected my wishes, but the challenge was on.

We always do some target shooting to reassure the hunter that his rifle is still shooting straight. And for me it is an opportunity to see whether the hunter can shoot. In this case the shooting at the target went very well, and we were able to begin the hunt.

It was Son's hunt, and I must say, it went very well. We had a lot of fun, walking and stalking most of the time. We also harvested some really fine trophies. Dad was only hunting for unique trophies or when the situation presented itself as a challenge. On the last day, Dad asked whether we could go back to the mountainous part of Otjisauona and hunt on the slopes for whatever might come our way. The setting sun was just touching the horizon when we eased over the top of a ridge. The gorge on the other side was narrow. And as we looked over to the opposite hillside, there was a large kudu bull watching us, about eighty yards away.

The moment we reached the top of the ridge he spotted us. Very quietly, but challenging me, Dad said, "What now? I do not have a bullet in the chamber!"

I replied, "Carefully chamber a round, move out behind me to my left, get on the sticks, and pull the trigger!"

He did exactly that and got a very nice kudu bull.

Peter Thormählen: One of my favorite clients is a female hunter who completed her whole Big Five with us. She and her husband are some of our premier clients, not because of the money they spend with us, but because they enjoy every little thing about Africa. It makes me ashamed sometimes to see that they notice little things that we miss most of the time as we are running around organizing safaris and guiding clients. On her third fourteen-day leopard safari in Namibia, we got her leopard. To see her joy, appreciation, and respect was a great experience. She and her husband will always be in our hunting memories.

Jamy Traut: I was about eighteen years old. We had to shoot a gemsbok for meat on a cattle farm in northeastern Namibia. The father of a friend had just bought himself a lever-action .44 Magnum and was very proud of it, and his son/my friend intended to join me for the weekend. This .44 was going along on our hunt as a backup gun to the .30-06, which had to do the main damage. We were given instructions to the extreme regarding how we must not scratch the new gun and how we should keep it in its case until really needed.

While we were sneaking up on a lone gemsbok, we spooked a young warthog. My friend decided that he wanted to shoot it with the lever-action. He gut-shot it, and the pig, after a few squeals, started circling like a spinning top. Angry, it then commenced what seemed to be a full-on charge, straight for my friend. I think my friend got off another shot, but as the little hog got closer, he decided that he better try to do some more damage in order to stop the "charge." The pig was approximately two yards away, and the time to reload was long past. What did my friend do? He hit the warthog smack on the head with the new gun, breaking the stock in half!

We did not get the gemsbok, and we were in all kinds of trouble when we got home. We have great memories, though.

Gerrit Utz: In 2007, I was guiding a longtime hunter of mine in Damaraland. His main goal was a Hartmann zebra. It was in November, and the first rains came early that year. We were driving in the remote part west of Leeukop when the trackers spotted some zebra at least eight hundred yards in front of us.

We left the vehicle behind and started to stalk them. About halfway there, we found out that they were two stallions together, which could not be

It's not unusual to start planning your second safari as your first one winds down. (Photo courtesy of Diethelm Metzger)

better! The wind was in our favor, and just an hour before we'd had rain, and all over were little ponds of water. The sandy ground between the rocks was very muddy.

We approached the two zebras and made it to about 140 yards behind a very small kopje. The hunter moved up and took the shot. We clearly heard the bullet hit, and when they ran off we saw the shot was a little too low and the front leg was broken. The zebra ran up a slope to a little plateau, but it was not possible for the hunter to get a second shot because of the bushes and rocks.

After a while, we went to the spot where they had been standing. The tracks were easy to see and follow. We tracked up the slope and up there we saw them slowly walking, disappearing on the other side of the plateau, but still together. We stalked to the other side, which was still three hundred yards, and found that all of a sudden the tracks were over a rocky flat plain, and going at full speed. We could not explain it because the wind was still fine, and they also had not seen us approaching. We followed the tracks, but as it got more sandy, we realized we were following only one zebra. They must have split up.

We returned to the gravel plain and found the injured one had turned to the left, but the one not wounded went straight on, both flat-out. We followed the wounded one, and after not even twenty yards we found the track of a single lion that was following the wounded zebra at a trot. Now the fun started.

We followed the track very carefully and after about a hundred yards, we looked down into a river and saw the zebra. The lion, which was nowhere in sight, had caught it and had already eaten part of it. We carefully checked every mopane bush around us for a distance of about thirty yards, but as hard as we looked, we were not able to find the lion. We were not brave enough to go closer to the zebra, and we had no more lion on quota. We slowly backed up, forced to accept our defeat at the paws of the lion.

The next day, the hunter took another zebra out of another stallion group with a single, perfect shot.

John Wambach: I was hunting elephants with a client who had been with me on two other trips and had become a close friend. After several days of following spoor and not getting a good bull, our morale was getting low. That morning we visited a water hole, looking for tracks, and we found the tracks of several bulls that had watered during the night. The trackers and I followed the tracks to sort out the direction the bulls had taken while Anneli, my fiancée then, followed in the truck with the client since the spoor followed the road from the water hole.

The trackers and I had gone some distance when we noticed that the truck had fallen behind and we could not see it any more, although we were still following the road. We stopped and waited, not knowing if there was a problem. After about ten minutes we suddenly heard the truck heading toward us at speed, and when we saw it there was a lot of motioning and what seemed like shouting, although we could not make out the sounds. The truck stopped in a cloud of dust and Anneli, the client, and the game scout were all talking and waving at the same time.

When we restored some order, we were told that there were bull elephants behind us and that the client had seen them. We all immediately grabbed what was necessary and took off after the elephants, finding where they had crossed the road behind us and took off on the spoor. We had not walked for much more than half an hour when we came upon them feeding.

We were trying to get a look at them when they must have sensed that we were there, for they started walking off at quite a pace. At that moment we spotted the bull that we had been looking for, but the others were now moving away from us at a pace that had us running behind them to keep up. Luckily, our bull moved to the side, allowing us to get close to him. As he moved through the high grass of a plain, we were fifteen yards off his tail.

Needless to say, it was incredible to have this bull right in front of us, not knowing whether he was going to turn around or charge. The bull started to turn to our right, and I got the client ready to take a side brain shot at the right time. The bull had his head cocked to his right, acknowledging our presence, but the wind stayed true, so he could only sense our movement.

Suddenly he turned and we had him with his head up, ears spread, fifteen yards in front of us. We froze as the client sighted, and at the shot the elephant's back legs dropped from under him as if he had stepped down a mine shaft.

After all the euphoria and nerves had settled, we then heard the full story of how the client had spotted the elephants: As we were tracking with the truck

Hunters usually pick up the tracks of elephants once they have left a water hole. Tracking may cover many miles.

following us, the client developed the need to answer the call of nature. Armed with a roll of toilet paper, he took to the bush quite a way from the truck, not wanting anybody to hear any of the embarrassing sounds.

As he lowered his breeches and squatted comfortably, it occurred to him that it would be pretty neat if an elephant walked by when he was in this position, and he chuckled at the picture in his mind. The very next moment, he heard some branches scratching against something, and there, forty yards away, a bull elephant walked out of the brush toward him.

Grabbing his breeches and not wanting to step in anything, he scurried for cover as he had no rifle with him. What a picture: hunter with breeches around ankles, wide-stepping through thorns and brush with exposed anterior, to get away from a totally oblivious elephant! Luckily, the elephant fed away from him, and he had time to get his pants on properly before making for the truck.

Sometimes we really have to be careful of what we ask for when on safari!